Traditions

Traditions

THE COMPLETE BOOK OF
PRAYERS, RITUALS, AND BLESSINGS
FOR EVERY JEWISH HOME

Sara Sherdelman and Dr. Avram Davis

NEW YORK

8

Introduction *8* – The Jewish Calendar *16*
Vocabulary of Jewish Values *18*

21

Part I: The Holiday Cycle

Rosh ha-Shanah *22* – The Ten Days of Awe *37* – Yom Kippur *40*
Sukkot *53* – Simchat Torah *63* – Hanukkah *70*
Tu Bi-Shevat *90* – Purim *95* – Pesah *104* – Counting the Omer *119*
Shavuot *124* – Tisha Be-Av *130*

137

Part II: Home Blessings

Shabbat *140* – Havdallah *155* – Blessings for Special Occasions *159*
New Rituals and Celebrations *176*

193

Part III: The Life Cycle

Naming *195* – Brit Milah *200* – Shiva *203*
Bar Mitzvah/Bat Mitzvah *207* – Ethical Will *222*

List of Contributors *227* – Kosher Foods *231*
Names of God *232* – New Family Traditions *233*
A List of Schools and Centers *235* – Bibliography *239*
Additional Readings *240* – Readings for Jewish Spiritual Practice *242*
Acknowledgments *244* – Dates of the Holidays: 1998-2002 *246*

When God prepared to give us our Torah, He/She wanted to be sure we knew how to use the precious gift. He/She asked who would be our guarantors. First we offered our holy patriarchs and matriarchs, and although we had received much merit from our forebears, God would not give us the Torah based on our past. We next offered our holy prophets, and although we had received much guidance from them, God also rejected these as a promise. Then we realized that the only way to assure the future of the Jewish people would be to offer our children as guarantors.

Thus God gathered all the children and babies and blessed them and made a mutual promise between the children and their parents and teachers that they would teach the sacred Torah to each other and down through all the generations.

L'dor va dor.

FROM GENERATION TO GENERATION
WE DEDICATE THIS BOOK
TO OUR CHILDREN, OUR HOLY TEACHERS,
ALIYA FLOREN SHENDELMAN DAVIS
AND
SHAENDL LEAH SHENDELMAN DAVIS
AND TO ALL OUR STUDENTS

The Wedding
by Leo Schutzman, Jewish Museum, New York.

The Jewish path is often called the Blessing Path, which is key to its understanding, and thus this book is ultimately about blessing. The tradition teaches us that we are expected to make a hundred blessings a day. Obviously, if we make a hundred blessings a day, there is very little time to be in any state other than "blessed." We are blessed by what we see and in turn we are asked to bless it. The nature of blessing is always reciprocal.

Introduction

For in order to be blessed by something or someone (and in turn to bless that thing or person), we must be *connected* to that person or object. And not merely connected, but in a state of *affectionate* or *compassionate* connection. It is very hard to be angry at our children, for example, when we are in the act of blessing them. It is very hard to sustain anger or sadness simultaneously with blessing. All acts of ritual are ultimately based on blessing. Blessing can be as simple as the recollection that after receiving a gift, we say thank you. Prayer is the statement of the opening heart—whether in need or in thanks. For all of us, daily life sometimes seems to be an obstacle course filled with rocks and thorns. The rituals and holidays of Judaism sometimes seem to be hopelessly encrusted by centuries of repetitions and naïve rules that cannot speak to modern people. But as the Bible says, there is

Deer of the Field
by Judith Hankin.

honey in the rock. There is *nourishment* of the sweetest kind, even in forms that seem stern and antiquated. This book, we hope, will help you find nourishment in the substance of blessing and ritual. It is a book of stories that will tell you where you might situate yourself in life, in this busy modern world, and how to help your children situate themselves as well. Ultimately all ritual is blessing—and blessing is an attempt to help stitch our individual lives into a greater fabric. For God weaves on a great loom, and every stitch links each individual soul to God's Soul and to millions of other stitches, other lives, other breaths. This book is a reflection of the Jewish life we have created in our home. A life that is filled with thankful attunement to the cycle of the seasons and the joy of sharing in like-minded community. For our children, the observance of the holiday cycle fills them so full of contentment that there is no longing for the customs of the larger society, especially in

December. Blessing is an actual tool or technique of inner transformation. It is meant to move us to a greater realization of Self and God. It is a concrete action, partaking both of psychology and the body and heart to influence the world to make *tikkun olam*, repair or healing. But saying this, we must also acknowledge that following rituals and traditions is not without danger. We may begin to repeat them mindlessly, simply out of force of habit, or from obligation, and in doing this we quickly lose our grip on the Divine and thus feel exiled from the land of meaning. But because the heart does not change, we will still yearn to belong and be part of the tapestry, and eventually we must return to the honey in the rock. For the hunger in our heart can only be filled with the mystery of the original blessing. The Jewish festival cycle reflects different moments in our lives and psyche. Properly observed, it can almost be a therapeutic model. At various times during the year we are called to examine our hearts and souls, make peace with our friends and family, celebrate our freedoms, give, receive, embrace nature, mourn, rejoice, and without limit contact our own spirituality, and reembrace our own existence. Blessing and rituals are like gateways into a world where we meet the Divine. There are gateways to holiness everywhere, but they are hidden by clever guardians who hold up mirrors that only reflect images of our laziness, boredom, sadness, depression, the feeling of emptiness ir our lives—these are clever obstacles to the gateway of holiness. When we come to the doorway, the guard holds up a mirror and tries to fool us with a reflection of our lazy spiritual attitude. "Why should I bother to perform a ritual?" we say to ourselves. This powerful reflection fools us and turns us away from the gateway. Indeed, the guard is clever, so we leave and never get to meet holiness. We come to another gateway and to another image held up for us in the mirror. Perhaps we say, "Oh well, these are just ancient, traditional words. They sound forced and empty to me. They served the tribe of Israel long ago, but they carry no meaning in my modern life." The guard has won again, and again we turn away. How many times are we going to be fooled by the clever guards? They are not

Pewter Presentation Plate,
1786, by Joseph Mitterbacher, Jewish Museum, New York.

really threatening, all they are doing is reflecting images of ourselves. We must go past these guards. Surrender ourselves to the ancient, almost shamanic power of the ritual. Rituals are ancient for a reason. They are ancient and long-lived because they *work*!

Ritual is an act. Sometimes ancient, but sometimes quite modern. Sometimes frozen in time, sometimes shifted to a very modern idiom. It is important to embrace ritual because blessing and ritual return us home, to unity, and to grace. This book presents an infinite variety of celebrating grace in everyday life, honoring the traditional holidays of the Hebrew calendar and individual life cycle, but also suggesting an array of spiritual practices that can be woven into ordinary days to render small moments extraordinary and significant. Every time we bless, every time we light a candle in ritual,

Wedding ring *from the Jewish Museum in New York.*

we embroider a stitch on the tapestry of God, enriching its colors, contributing to the design and strengthening the weave. This is the ancestral tradition that will enrich the memories of our children, family, community, and friends. Life is nothing, after all, but a series of small moments, and if we can be present for those then we are blessed indeed. The book is divided into three main parts: "The Holiday Cycle," "Home Blessings," and "The Life Cycle." In each part you will find both traditional and reform material to enrich your life, some of which will be elaborate and ancient, some passionate and inspiring. The Holy Days described in Part 1 follow the traditional Hebrew calendar. Under each heading you will find sections on the meaning of the holiday, the traditions and customs, the synagogue observance, the home observance, blessings and prayers, ritual objects, food, modern expansions, and a few thoughts on the psychological preparation that makes us ready to embrace a holy moment. Part 2, "Home Blessings" is orchestrated around family activities that can be done by children and adults together—such cooperation will create a magical atmosphere in the home and unite the family in a very special way. Children will awaken ancestral memories as they play and prepare for rituals. And finally, "The Life Cycle" concentrates on honoring those moments of life that are private and centered on the home and covers a number of life-cycle events that are observed communally with the help of a rabbi.

The main emphasis throughout the book is on creating personal rituals for spiritual and emotional awakening that help us find the honey in the rock-strewn paths of our lives. The hope is to provide images, methods, and practices that are steps toward wholeness and that answer the need in each one of us to find nourishment for our soul within the tradition we were born into. Blessings and rituals are the supporting foundations of a meaningful life, upon which we build ladders that lead us to immortality. Spirituality today is not just for inspiration but is an absolute necessity for the wholeness of God's tapestry and the essential integrity of our world and our children's world. This book is not only for Jews. We think of Judaism as a great table laden with delicacies. All people are invited to this feast. Come, have a nibble, use what is good for you. Take it with you to some other table, if that is your desire. Or stay, and partake fully of the feast. Whichever suits you. This book offers a host of delicacies of blessing. We suspect that the Jewish community is moving into what we call a post-denominational period. That is, an increasing number of people observe a mix of customs. Some of these are orthodox, some conservative, some popular. Everyone is a cultural mix. This mix is profoundly American, and as such it is profoundly exciting, for we are becoming a truly native, American Judaism. What all of its parameters are is not yet clear. But it is a passionate, hands-on version, embracing old disciplines like meditation, as well as rituals such as those found in this book. We bless all who use this book with the joy of Torah and with the deep insight provided by loving, spiritual community.

-SARA SHENDELMAN AND AVRAM DAVIS, BERKELEY, ELUL 5757

Remember the days of old

He found him in the wilderness land

He set him upon the high places of the earth

That he might eat the yield of the land

That he might suckle honey from the rock

-DEUTERONOMY 32:7, 10, 13

The Jewish Calendar

Untitled
by Shonna Husbands-Hankin.

All Jewish holidays begin at sundown on the eve of the holiday. All holidays are dated by the days and months of the Hebrew calendar and they are different from the general (European) calendar. The Hebrew calendar is based on twelve twenty-eight-day cycles of the moon, which adds up to 336 days in a year. The general calendar is based on the yearly cycle of the earth around the sun, which takes 365 days. Because the moon cycle is shorter than the sun cycle, to make up the difference an additional month called Adar Bet ("Adar Two") is added periodically to the Jewish calendar. There is another main difference between the Hebrew and the general calendars: the years of the Hebrew calendar are counted from the Biblical reckoning of the creation of the world nearly 6,000 years ago, while the general calendar counts the years from the birth of Christ. The year 1998 of the general calendar is the year 5759. You can find the season and month of each Jewish holiday on the chart opposite. And to see on what days holidays will fall in the following years, please refer to the section entitled "Dates of the Holidays: 1998-2002."

SEASON	EUROPEAN MONTH	HEBREW MONTH	HOLIDAY
Fall	September October November	Elul Tishri Hershvan	Rosh ha-Shanah Ten Days of Awe Yom Kippur Sukkot Simchat Torah
Winter	December January February	Kislev Tevet Shevat	Hanukkah Tu Bi-Shevat
Spring	March April May	Adar (Adar Bet) Nisan Iyyar	Purim Passover Holocaust Remembrance Day Pesah Israel Independence Day Lag Ba-Omer
Summer	June July August	Sivan Tammuz Av	Shavuot Tisha Be-Av

Vocabulary of Jewish Values

Although every element of the Jewish tradition speaks to a different part of the Jewish soul, there is no injunction more important than that regarding the way we relate to each other as human beings. In the *V'ahavta* part of the *K'riat Sh'ma* we are enjoined to teach our children by our own daily example. Below is a list of *midot*, Jewish values, that help us treat each other humanly in what Martin Buber called an "I-thou" relationship. These values give us some guidelines and a context for the foundations of our spiritual community. You can read these as a private meditation and then apply them when relating with your family and community as a form of daily spiritual practice.

Bal Tashchit Mitzvah of not destroying or being wasteful

Bikkur Cholim Mitzvah of visiting the sick

Bushah Causing embarrassment

Chesed Mercy, compassion, or loving-kindness

Chevre The community of spiritual seekers

Chesed Shel Emet Mitzvah of caring for the dead

Davven Prayer, usually communal

Devekut Rapturous attachment; a state of mind cultivated in Jewish meditation

Ein Sof One of the names of God. Literally the "without end." It is the idea of God-as-process, rather than as an object

Essen Tag Home hospitality on holidays for the poor

Gemilut Chasadim Deeds of loving-kindness

Gemilut Shel Chesed Free loan (no interest)

Gilgul ha-Nefesh Reincarnation

Hachnasat Kallah Mitzvah of providing a dowry for a bride

Hachnasat Orchim Mitzvah of hospitality

Halbashat Arumin Mitzvah of clothing those in need

Hashgacha Pratit Divine providence

Hekdesh Community shelter for those in need

Hitbodedut Usually defined as inner-directed meditation

Hitbonenut Usually defined as outer-directed meditation

Kavod Mitzvah of granting honor or dignity

Kavvanah Focused, passionate intentionality

Keren Ami Means "fund of my people," refers to monetary gifts collected in religious schools

Kavod Z'keynim Mitzvah of honoring the elderly

Kuppah Community Tzedakah fund

Leket Remains of harvesting left for the poor; gleaning

Ma'aser 10-percent tithe for the poor

Ma'ot Chittin Mitzvah of providing Passover foods for the poor

Mashpiah Spiritual director

Matanot L'Evyonim Gifts to the poor on Purim

Mazon Mitzvah of providing food for the hungry

Mench/Menchlikite Being a good person; living in the image of God

Mochin Gadlut "Great mind," enlightenment

Musar Development of personal qualities, a prerequisite for deep-meditation practice

Nichum Avaylim Comforting the mourners

Peah Corner of the field that must be left for the poor

Pidyon Sh'vuylin Mitzvah of freeing the captives

Pushke Tzedakah box

Rachamim Mercy, compassion

Tamchul Community soup kitchen

Tefillah Prayer and/or meditation

Tikkun Olam Fixing, repairing the world

Tsadik A righteous person

Tzedakah Monetary gifts to help those in need

Tzedek Justice

בה
זה השער לײי צדיקים
יבאו בו ׃

סדר הגדה
של פסח

עם פירוש יפה בלשון חכמים ׃ וציר צבורים טבעיים נחים
מהא'הת והפתשים ׃ כמנהג הקבלה לאבותינו במצרים ׃
ותורת בית המקדש תוצב אכ׳ד הכלכתבתע׳ד מהש עלקלי
נח׳ת בדיו יפה ונכתב בדפוס

אמשטרדם

ונכתב פה ק׳ק פיורדא אצל גירנבורג לסדר
ולפרט אשרי אדם מצא ה ח ה והורע
דרך במלאנת הקדש למק

PART I

The Holiday Cycle

Rosh ha-Shanah:
THE GRACE OF NEW BEGINNINGS

*Sound on the new moon the shofar, at the darkening of the moon, the day of
our festival; for it is a statute for Israel, a ruling of the God of Jacob.*
−PSALM 81:4−5

The High Holidays mark one of the Jewish New Years—the birthday of the world—consisting of a holiday cycle that begins with
Rosh ha-Shanah—the New Year—on the first two days of the
month of Tishri and ends with the Day of Atonement—Yom
Kippur—on the tenth of Tishri. The days between these two festivals have also become part of the cycle and are called in Hebrew
Yamim Noraim—Days of Awe.

This long cycle of holy days is a time of profound renewal; it
marks the end of the old year, from time immemorial a symbol of
death and rebirth, is followed by the Days of Awe, and culminates
with introspection and a personal and collective analysis of the
great themes of human life linked to the passing of time: who we
are, where we come from, where we are going. In ancient agrarian
cycles autumn was a period of harvests and of preparation for the
winter months to come, a time of spiritual indwelling, when
nature all around us would display a last burst of color before

Judith Hankin.

slowing down to the cold of winter. Because of our inborn sensitivity to the changes in our environment, this is a time when we feel instinctually introspective and when spiritual renewal is the natural reflection of the changes occurring in the outer world. At this time of year we are able to draw on energies that are stored deep within our being and that form our spiritual reservoir, giving us strength and nourishment. In times past, autumn was the time when granaries were stocked up high with grains to sustain families throughout the winter. Think of this as a spiritual metaphor: a time for stocking up on Godliness to sustain us for the year ahead. The length of the holy days is also appropriate, for we need time to come to terms with our relationship with God, cleanse the bond with the divine and with the community from our wrongdoing, and reenter the mystery of renewal.

Rosh ha-Shanah marks the seventh, and thus a very special, new moon. This is the New Year of Israel, a time of renewal that is heralded by the blowing of the *shofar,* the ram's horn, whose sounds alerted Israel to God's close presence on Sinai before the Covenant was forged. The New Year is celebrated on the first two days of Tishri (Reform Jews only celebrate the first day) and marks the anniversary of the creation of the world. The most important place for the observance of Rosh ha-Shanah is the synagogue and not the home, and the liturgy's most relevant

Shofar Horn, *from Russia, nineteenth century.*

theme is that of God as King—*melekh*—the One who in the beginning created the world and that the creation continues to unfold. Rosh ha-Shanah is at the same time the end of one cycle and the beginning of another. This is a time when we open to the grace of new beginnings, when we can progress through the great power of the King and the small things in our lives can melt into His creation.

Because Rosh ha-Shanah falls on the seventh new moon, there has always been a little confusion for the worldwide Jewish community in comprehending the starting times of the New Year. The practical solution was found, therefore, to add two days to the celebrations (Reform Jews only celebrate for one day).

Meaning

It has been suggested by Rabbi Yehuda Aryeh Lei
Rosh ha-Shanah actually refers to the state of bei
differentiation of the divine emanation into sepa:
with this original state of formless being that we make contact
again on Rosh ha-Shanah, aided by the soundless words of the
shofar. Rosh ha-Shanah in the Torah was originally called *Yom
Teruah*, which literally means the "Day of Sounding the *Shofar*."
It was not called the New Year until Talmudic times.

The sounds of the *shofar* are symbolically intended to awaken
us from the unconsciousness that may have developed during
the previous year. The New Year gives us a chance to become
conscious again, to renew our connection with God
and existence.

Traditions and Customs

The month before Rosh ha-Shanah—Elul—is a
time to get ready for the festive period. The
shofar is sounded at the end of every morning synagogue service, its extraordinary
sound awaking the community to
the important time ahead.
Sound stirs the emotions,
and the ancient *shofar* provides a response in us to
the mystery celebrated at
the New Year. Elul is a
time of culmination—when people go to their family graves and
remember the past before moving towards the new. Ready to
begin the New Year, we give our thoughts to others, and we send
out cards of good fortune. As Rosh ha-Shanah comes close,

...ryone prepares—the annual ark covers and the cover of the reading table are set aside. The white covers are used instead, symbolizing purity. The men by tradition go to the *mikveh*—the ritual bath.

The most important ritual of Rosh ha-Shanah, occurring during the synagogue ceremonies, is the sounding of the *shofar.* This was the ram's horn sounded on Mount Sinai when the people of Israel first felt the presence of God.

There are three *shofar* sounds—*tekiah,* which is one long blast; *shevarim,* three short blasts; and *teruah,* nine staccato blasts.

The sound of the *shofar* is a blessing—the blessing of awakening, and new beginnings. At the sound of the shofar, the *Utaneh Tokef* hymn is sung, describing the deep feelings experienced by humanity when facing God who stands in judgment over us all.

Another important part of Rosh ha-Shanah centers on the Book of Life. Tradition tells us that God holds both the Book of Life and the Book of Death. In these books, every individual's name is written. This is symbolic of endings and beginnings, of the realization that our lives are frail and dependent on powers greater than us. The realization of vulnerability helps us to receive the gift of life from God.

Rosh ha-Shanah plate,
Jewish Museum, New York.

Symbols

Rosh ha-Shanah is the birthday of the world. It honors the creation of the universe and spinning of the weave of time that binds
us all together. There also exists a Jewish tradition that deems
Rosh ha-Shanah not to be the beginning of the world but the
beginning of human life in the world, and thus the beginning of
the long and intimate relationship between God and His people.
Thus, as well as honoring new beginnings, Rosh ha-Shanah celebrates the importance of human life as the receptacle of divine
love. History, blessing and rituals began when Adam took the
first steps into the Garden that was created for him. In accord
with both traditions, the Torah reading chosen at the synagogue
for Rosh ha-Shanah is not the story of creation (Gen. 1:1) but the
stories of the birth of Isaac and the birth of Samuel—both
accounts telling of new life born from barrenness.

On the first day of Rosh ha-Shanah, we read in scripture the
story of Sarah giving birth to Isaac. The figure of Sarah is central
to the meaning of Rosh ha-Shanah—she is an old barren woman
married to an old man who hears three mysterious men outside
her tent predict that she will become pregnant. She laughs at the
absurdity, even though she believes in God and divine prophecy.
When she does become pregnant, she names her son Isaac which
means "laughter." New beginnings are always unexpected. They
occur at a threshold where the old is passing away and we don't yet
know what is going to happen. In fact we may think that life is
coming to an end, like Sarah, who, believing that before her was
only death, was stunned to learn she was with child. There is little
we can do to prepare for the unexpected, except to honor and
celebrate the ebb and flow of life through our bodies, hearts, and
spirits. This is perhaps the deeper meaning of Rosh ha-Shanah—
one of opening, and allowing the hand of God do its works
through us.

Rituals

As mentioned before, Rosh ha-Shanah is rooted in the communal, synagogue experience. But there are a number of folk and family customs. Even as we begin the period where we stand in judgment, we celebrate life: we light candles, we dip apples and hallah in honey (sweetness upon sweetness), and, of course, we have a festive meal with blessings from family and friends. It is the tradition on Rosh ha-Shanah afternoon to go to a body of living water (stream, ocean, river), and symbolically cast out our failings by throwing bread crumbs into the water. This act is called *tashlikh* in Hebrew, and it is symbolic of renewal. The ceremony may be accompanied by a reading of Micah 7:18-20, Psalm 118:5-9, and Psalms 13 and 130. Among these, in particular, the verse "You will cast your sins into the depths of the sea" (Mic. 7:19) helps us articulate the symbolic significance of the ceremony.

Judaism often seeks to ground the mystical in a very concrete action. The simple act of standing by a body of water and dissolving our heavy load is wonderfully powerful. Another custom is to gather and recall the times we have succeeded in our tasks during the year and remember projects that we hope to succeed in during the coming year.

Jewish New Year Banner, *1942-43,*
undyed silk, Jewish Museum, New York.

Arts and Crafts

One of the ways to prepare children and adults alike for the cele-brations of the High Holy Days is to make cards at home. You can make these either by employing traditional papercut designs that are photocopied and colored in by the children, or by making up original cards using your unique talents. The writing on the cards can itself be a source of both learning and inspiration, through quotes of biblical passages or personal messages updating family on the recent events of your life. Making holiday cards is a won-derful family activity in which everyone can participate. In these pages you will find illustrations of sample cards to inspire you. You can copy some of these designs and adapt them for your per-sonal use, or draw new ones born from your imagination. Honor Rosh ha-Shanah to all those you know around the world.

Like An Apple Tree
by Judith Hankin.

Rosh ha-Shanah Dessert

DRIED FRUIT TSIMMES
12-16 SERVINGS PAREVE

This dense, sweet fruit compote can be used at any holiday during the year. I always start out the year with this dish. My Aunt Frieda always served it at her holiday table, and we have taken it into our family's table.

ASSORTED DRIED FRUITS:

1 lb. apricots
3 lb. pitted prunes
Other dried fruits, such as pears, dried apples, nectarines, etc.
1 cup whole pecans or walnuts
1 sliced lemon
1 sliced orange
2 cinnamon sticks

Use any combination of fruits that you like, taking care not to use fruit that will disintegrate when cooked for a long time. Remember, this is really stewed fruit.

Put all fruit in a large saucepan and cover with water. Add cinnamon sticks and cloves. Bring to a boil and then reduce heat to a simmer. Add the sliced lemon and orange. After the mixture has cooked for about 15 minutes, add the nuts. Stir occasionally to keep from sticking. Cook until the liquid is syrupy, but not dry. Serve cold or at room temperature. Can be stored for a month in the refrigerator, if kept well covered.

Kavvanot—Meditations:
Modern Expansions and Personal Preparation

If we imagine that the end of a cycle is like a narrow crack between two rocks through which we must pass in order to reach the landscape of newness, then the New Year—that magical time of change, transformation, and renewal—is about letting go of everything that will prevent us from passing through that narrow crack. It is about shedding old attitudes that we keep but that no longer serve us when relating to others, about ridding ourselves of old remorse, anger, frustration. The New Year is a wondrous opportunity for cleaning one's spiritual house: review what is weighing on your spirit and let it go, die with the old. If you do this as spiritual practice you will enter the morning of Rosh ha-Shanah completely renewed and bathed in a fresh glow of light, like a dewdrop on an autumn morning.

The process of renewal and cleansing starts from the individual and extends to the social: honor your friends and loved ones one by one, thinking of them and meeting them individually. Make time to renew your bond with each one and gift them with a few very personal and intimate moments. These are the moments of blessing when, together, we do nothing but be together, feeling each other, and speaking gently from the heart. This is the most wonderful grace of new beginnings.

BLESSING FOR THE APPLE AND HONEY

Praised are You, Lord our God, King of the Universe,
who creates the fruit of the tree.

Glossary of Terms and Traditions of Interest

Apples and honey The evening before Rosh ha-Shanah, before the festival lights are lit and before the kiddush is recited, traditionally a piece of apple is dipped in honey. *She-he-heyanu* is spoken and the words *May it be God's will to grant us a good and a sweet year* are also spoken. On the second night of the festival it is also a custom to eat a fruit that is not one common to the prior season and then recite the *She-he-heyanu* once again.

Ba'al Tokayah The person who sounds the shofar during the High Holy Day period: literally means "Master of the Telziah."

Kittel A white garment worn on the Holy Days that represents purity and is a symbol of Jewish faith.

L'shanah tovah tikatayvu "May you be sealed for a good year." The Rosh ha-Shanah greeting that is given to all those who are met and that offers the hope that the other will be sealed in The Book of Life—a gesture that guarantees joy in the coming year.

Rosh ha-Shanah Literally, "Head of the Year."

Shevarim One of the sounds made by the *shofar*, consisting of three short broken notes

Shofar An instrument made from the horn of a ram. It is sounded every morning during Elul, on the morning of Rosh ha-Shanah, and at the conclusion of Yom Kippur.

Tekiah One of the sounds of the *shofar*, consisting of one deep note that ends abruptly.

Tekiah gedolah A long *tekiah*.

Teruah Another of the sounds of the *shofar,* consisting of nine short broken notes that make a wavering sound.

Yamim Noraim "Days of Awe": the ten days beginning with Rosh ha-Shanah and ending with Yom Kippur. First used in the Middle Ages, the expression described both the sense of horror at the persecutions of the time and the awe for God.

Blessings

The traditional greetings for Rosh ha-Shanah are *Shanah tovah* ("A good year") or *Le-shanah tovah u-metukah tikateivu* ("May you be inscribed for a good and sweet year"). The blessing of Rosh ha-Shanah is in a new beginning, and before blessing others one should contemplate what the meaning of a new beginning is within the context of a particular life. What is this new beginning for me today? Rabbi Schachter-Shalomi expresses the following thoughts on the blessing of starting a new page in the Book of Life:

> *...improve your deeds. I must examine the issues in my life to discover which changes are necessary, because without them my life is too terrible to live. Unless I write myself into the Book of Life, I am certainly not going to live for another year. I must renew my will to live. Each of us must try to write a page in the Book of Life, consisting of what we desire in the coming year.*
>
> -MICHAEL STRASSFELD

Following are some of the traditional blessings for
Rosh ha-Shanah:

*Praised are You, God, Ruler of the Universe, for granting us life, for sustaining us,
and for helping us to reach this day.*

Baruch, Ata, Adonai Eloheinu, sheheyann, I kiyamanu, vhigiyanu lazman hazeh.

Kiddush for Rosh ha-Shanah Morning

*Blessed are You, Lord our God, Ruler of the
Universe, Who has sanctified us with
His commandments and com-
manded us to kindle the light of
the festival.*

*Baruch Atah, Adonai
Eloheinu, Melekh Haolim,
asher kidshanu b'mitzvotav,
i'tzivanu lehadlik ner shel
yom tov.*

Blessing Bowl
by Susan Felix.

35

TRANSITION

Be quiet, my soul, be quiet.
Let the waves take you one by one
and sail you to the crescent of the moon.

Yes, the world is roaring
and there is work to do...
but to-night, my soul, to-night is yours
to behold
the beauty of the december sunset
as the year prepares to yield
and take its place in history.
        –MONIQUE PASTERNAK

T'SHUVAH

Like ripe fruits
our lives have fallen back to earth
to release their seeds on the spiral of time.
As we lie awake in the dark tunnels of turning,
the electric nights of Elul tear
at our flesh; in the morning
the sound of the shofar
our sole link to memory
breaks the air and calls the soul.
For 40 days and 40 nights
we waver, suspended, until
naked in its promise the seed stands
and the spark of judgment returns
to ignite our life.
        –MONIQUE PASTERNAK

The Ten Days of Awe

The ten days between Rosh ha-Shanah and Yom Kippur are meant to be a time of introspection that makes them a biblically divergent holiday with the thematic unity of transformation of the High Holiday process called *aseret yemei teshuvah*—the ten days of repentance. This is the period when the unrighteous can still repent and be written into the Book of Life. It is a time of mitigation and deep inner work. For example, it is necessary to go to those we have wronged and make our peace. The way the divine is experienced is through compassion and reconciliation.

This is a time of increased passion—passion for self-truth, self-knowledge, and making peace with ourselves, our loved ones and the world through an introspective period of deep prayer and meditation. Though an introspective time, it is extremely active psychologically.

Tzom Gedaliah

In antiquity, Gedaliah was the last Jewish Govenor of Judea.
He was appointed by the Babalonians to rule the remnant of the
Jewish State after the destruction of the First Temple (586 B.C.E.).
His assassination was the essential end of Jewish soverenity. Except
for brief periods until Pre-Roman times.

Shonna Husbands-Hankin.

Yom Kippur:
AT-ONE-MENT

Yom Kippur ends the ten days of *teshuvah* (return) begun on Rosh
ha-Shanah. It is intended to leave us feeling that we face our
mortality cleansed, renewed, and filled with purpose. We read in
the Torah that God gave Moses specific instructions for the
"Sabbath of Sabbaths." It is a time very much about us as individuals, and our place in the community, the essence of which is said
in the teaching of Hillel—"Do not do to others what is hateful to
yourself." In order to enhance our throughtfulness and focus our
attention, we fast, stop working, wear white and no leather, do
not bathe, and have no sexual relations.

All activity is in the synagogue, where there are services most
of the day.

Kol Nidrei Evening service.

Shaharit The morning service including Torah service and Yizkor.

Musaf A service which includes the martyrology and the *Avodah*.

Minhah Afternoon service which includes the Book of Jonah.

Neilah Just before sundown. We push our prayers through the
closing gates.

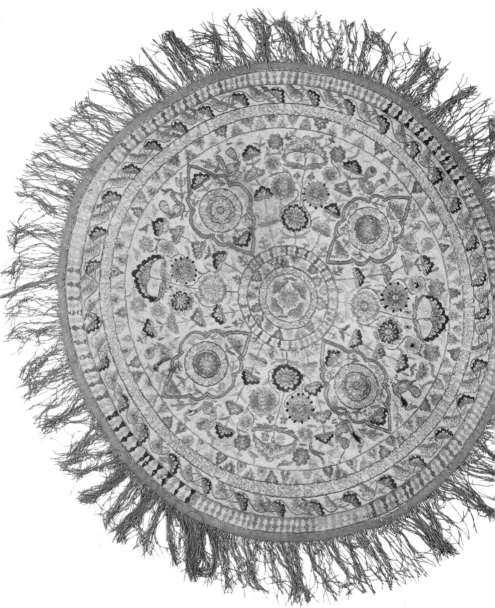

Cotton Sabbath Cloth, *1806, embroidered with polychrome silk, Jewish Museum, New York.*

Traditions and Customs

EREV YOM KIPPUR

The day before Yom Kippur is a special time of preparation.

One of the old customs is *kapparot* (atonements), which involved taking a rooster or hen and twirling it around the head, reciting a prayer that the chicken be killed instead of the individual who performed the ceremony. Today, instead of twirling the chicken and then killing it, money in a handkerchief can be substituted.

In the afternoon is the last meal before the fast, called the *seudah ha-mafseket.* Wishing others a *tzom kal*— an easy fast—is traditional.

Here we light the holiday candles with the blessing and *She-he-heyanu.* We also light a special memorial candle to burn throughout Yom Kippur in memory of deceased parents, and we bless our children. The table is covered with a special holiday cloth, which is usually white, and all the family dress in white also.

Mizrach, *a decoration hung on synagogue or home wall to show direction of prayer, facing west towards Jerusalem, from Poland. 1882. Israel Museum, Jerusalem.*

SYNAGOGUE OBSERVANCE

The evening service begins with *Kol Nidrei*—one of the best-known prayers in the liturgy. The chanting is intended to void any promises we have made that we will be unable to keep in the coming year. A Torah scroll is held on either side of the service leader. *Kol Nidrei* is then chanted three times before sundown. This tradition dates from fifteenth-century Spain.

On Yom Kippur also, a prayer shawl is worn for *Kol Nidrei* and for all the services. Some may wish to take off leather shoes for services.

Following *Kol Nidrei* is the *Ma'ariv* service. All services have special High Holiday *nusach* (melody) different for each service. The next morning there is the *Shaharit*, then the memorial prayer for the dead, called *Yizkor*, is normally read after the Torah reading, though some congregations move it to later in the afternoon, timed during this part of the day because those who have not suffered a loss may not wish to attend.

Included in the Yom Kippur davening are the *Avodah* service and the martyrology. In temple times the *Avodah* involved sacrifices and a series of confessions by the

Aleinu, *papercut by Judith Hankin.*

high priest. This service was the origin of the term "scapegoat," as a goat was taken to the desert and sacrificed to bring atonement for Israel's sins.

In making his confession, the High Priest would go for one day in the year to the Holy of Holies, where he would pronounce the name of God, which is not said today, mainly because no one knows any longer how to pronounce it. An important custom arose out of this tradition, where everyone first drops to the knees and then the body is stretched outwards with the head almost touching the ground in complete prostration at the speaking of the name of God. After the *Avodah* there is the martyrology. The reason for this is to tell the story of the martyrs killed by the Romans. Today some prayer books include material related to the Holocaust as well. There is no morbid purpose to this, but simply a reminder of the power of the faith.

The final service—*Neilah*—of Yom Kippur acquires its name and much of its content from the symbol of heaven's gates closing. Originally the term probably related to the closing of the temple gates, and is an energetic service said while standing.

Finally comes the sound of the *shofar*—the central symbol of the High Holidays. This ends the day and the whole period of Yom Kippur.

Yom Kippur Recipes

KREPLACH

6-8 SERVINGS MEAT

(This dish may be made Pareve or Dairy, depending on the meat substitute used)

It is traditional to eat kreplach before the Yom Kippur fast. The following recipe can be made with the traditional meat filling, or with a vegetarian substitute. My son Daniel loves kreplach.

WONTON NOODLE WRAPPERS

(available at most grocery stores in the fresh produce section)

MEAT OR SUBSTITUTE FILLING

1 medium onion, chopped fine
³/₄ cup ground meat, or ground meat substitute (available in many grocery stores)
1 egg
Salt and pepper to taste

Sauté the onion with the ground meat or substitute. Remove any excess fat. Combine with egg, salt and pepper to taste. Open wonton wrapper, and remove one noodle sheet at a time. Keep others covered with a damp towel. Place 1 tbsp. on each square. Follow directions on package for sealing wonton. Fold into a triangle and press edges together firmly. Leave as is, or press together two of the ends. Drop into boiling water and cook uncovered for 15 minutes. After being formed, kreplach can be placed on a cookie sheet and frozen.

They can be used in traditional chicken soup, or to create a special vegetarian soup.

VEGETARIAN BROTH
10-12 SERVINGS PAREVE

Kreplach or matzo balls can be served in this lovely, flavorful broth. Three of my four children are vegetarians. Ariel particularly enjoys this soup with matzo balls.

USE A LARGE SELECTION OF VEGETABLES, INCLUDING:

Carrots
Celery
Onions
Parsnips
White potatoes
Sweet potatoes
Tomatoes
Cabbage
Rutabaga
Potatoes, regular and sweet
Dill and other herbs
Bay leaves
Parsley
And any other vegetables you want

Put the whole vegetables in a large stock pot and cover with water. Bring to a boil, and then reduce heat. Cook for at least 4 hours or until vegetables are soft. Press vegetables in a sieve over a pot. Save the liquid and discard the vegetables. You can save the carrots to slice into the broth. Add salt and pepper to taste.

Yom Kippur Story

RETOLD BY DANIEL LEV

The essential practice of Yom Kippur is called Teshuva. *Although the word is usually translated as "repentance," its literal meaning is more relevant to modern concerns over relationship difficulties, addictive behavior, and other hurtful actions. Literally,* Teshuva *means "to turn around." When we make* Teshuva *we try to turn our life around, to turn it away from the destructive path it has been on and forge a new one toward a holy life. Sometimes when we do this we have to leave behind a whole part of ourselves, a part that has been destroying us. The following story teaches us this truth.*

One day, not too far from the awesome holiday of Yom Kippur, the Day of Atonement, Michol the Hood came to see the Chassidic master Elimelech of Lizensk. Now Michol had been the head of a very profitable and feared Jewish mafia that operated in nineteenth-century Eastern Europe. He had committed every crime imaginable but was now in midlife and felt the pangs of regret for the life that he had led. He had no wife, children, or family to speak of, and it had been years since he had stepped into a synagogue. Despite his evil life, Michol was still a Jew and felt drawn to change his ways and seek redemption through the practice of *Teshuva*. He desperately wanted to be forgiven by God for all of the evil he had wrought.

So it was that he now brought himself to the great Rebbe Elimelech. Surely the master could help him gain forgiveness for all of his sins. The Rebbe knew of Michol and told him to go home and turn all of his material wealth into cash, place it in a white bag, and return with it in three days. Michol did so, and in three days brought back a huge bag stuffed with thousands of rubles. The Rebbe told him to drop it on the table and sit down. There Michol found a paper and quill pen. Reb Elimelech instructed him in a stern voice to make a complete list of every sin he had committed since his Bar Mitzvah. Grimly, Michol carried out the Rebbe's task, finishing it in three hours, filling twelve pages front and back.

The Rebbe instructed Michol to stand before him as he read the list out loud: "Oy Gevalt, Michol, how could you do this and this and this...and you treated this old woman horribly and this is what you did to that little girl..." The Rebbe read on and on in ever-increasing volume and incredulity until Michol became so filled with guilt, remorse, and tension that he fainted dead away. Reb Elimelech went to his kitchen, returned with a glass of water, and threw it in Michol's face. When the repentant came to, the Rebbe got him on his feet and continued the reading of the list of sins. Michol fainted ten more times before the list was finished.

"Oh Rebbe, please," begged Michol the Hood, "tell me what I have to do in order to make a complete *Teshuva* and be forgiven by heaven."

Reb Elimelech thought for a long time and then spoke: "In the days of the Beyt ha-Mlkdash, the Holy Temple, someone with such a list of crimes could not be forgiven in this life. The only way to receive forgiveness was in death, and the way of death was by swallowing a spoon of molten lead. This is the only way you can be forgiven."

Michol sat very still for some time while the Rebbe waited. Finally, he sadly nodded his head, "If this is the only way, then I will sub-mit to the will of heaven." So strong was his determination to change that he was will-ing to do so in death.

"Here's what you must do," said the Rebbe. "Take a few rubles from the bag and go out and buy a metal spoon, a small chunk of lead, some flux, and a small towel. Bring it here by tonight."

When Michol returned he found his master stoking a huge fire in the fireplace in his study. He beckoned Michol over and began to instruct him: "Place the lead and flux in the spoon. . . now hold the towel at the end of the spoon and melt the lead over the fire."

In performing this action, Michol felt the deep sense of surrender and devotion that was experienced by the ancient Temple priests. Throughout the procedure, he offered up his life as a priest would offer up a repentance sacrifice.

The Rebbe took the spoon and told Michol to lie down on the floor before the fire. He lead him through the *Vidui*, the confessional prayer said before death. Then he said the *Shema* prayer attesting to the oneness of God. He then covered Michol's eyes with a kerchief. In his heart, Michol was prepared to give over his soul to God.

"Now, Michol, prepare to receive the judgment and forgiveness of heaven," thundered Reb Elimelech. He then put a spoon into Michol's open mouth...and...Michol...felt...marmalade, sweet, orange marmalade squishing around in his mouth. He sat up, confused, his eyes pleading with the Rebbe for understanding.

"You are no longer Michol. Michol is dead and completely forgiven." Said Reb Elimelech in the most gentle voice, "You are a new soul in Israel. Find a new name, take this bag of money, and go out to do good in the world."

And so it was.

Sabbath candlesticks from Russia,
eighteenth century, silver, Jewish Museum, New York.

Glossary of Terms and Traditions of Interest

Book of Jonah Read on the afternoon of Yom Kippur, this is the story of a prophet who flees, and then returns to God's service. It speaks of God's forgiveness for all.

G'mar chatimah tovah A greeting used between Rosh ha-Shanah and Yom Kippur, it means "Be sealed (in the Book of Life) for good."

Kol Nidrei One of the best known prayers of Yom Kippur and means "All vows." It is chanted at the beginning of the *Ma'ariv* service on the evening of Yom Kippur.

Tallit A prayer shawl usually used only for morning worship.

Teshuva "Returning" to our best selves. It indicates that we turn away from those behaviors that interfere with our own spirituality and godliness.

Vidui The Jewish Confession, made directly to God without the aid of any intermediary.

Yom Kippur Literally, "Day of Atonement."

Avram Davis.

Sukkah decoration, *by Israel David Luzzatto, Italy, 1833,*
in ink and watercolor on paper, Jewish Museum, New York.

Sukkot:

HAVEN OF PEACE

Sukkot, also known as the Fall harvest holiday—*hag-ha-asif*, or "festival of in-gathering"—occupies the seven days from Tishri 15 to 21. It is a holiday of joy after Yom Kippur, when we all enter into the spirit of Sukkot.

Sukkot continues the story of the Israelites, which began with the Exodus from Egypt (Passover) and the giving of the Torah at Sinai (Shavuot). Traditionally there were three pilgrimage festivals —Sukkot, Pesah, and Shavuot. For each one, a different phase of an agricultural cycle is celebrated, and on this holiday we build huts in the practice of the workers during harvests when they lived in temporary huts in the fields. The tradition also reminds us of when we lived as desert people.

Sukkot is called *zeman simhateinu*—the season to rejoice. We are commanded to be happy, and the holiday is a meditation of focusing on joy, and putting aside our worries.

Originally pilgrims came from all over Israel to Jerusalem to take part in the temple rites of Sukkot, perhaps their most important festival of all the biblical and Temple periods. Sukkot is also the festival of the future, for, according to tradition, in the messianic period all the nations of the world will assemble in Jerusalem and celebrate together.

Traditions and Customs

THE *SUKKAH*

You shall live in huts seven days; all citizens of Israel shall live in huts, in order that future generations may know that I made the Israelite people live in huts when I brought them out of the land of Egypt, I the Lord your God.

-LEV. 23:42, 4JL

For most people, Sukkot is about building a *sukkah.* The *sukkah* is a temporary tent-like dwelling usually made with a roof of branches. It must be finished in the four days before the holiday, and we use it for the first time on the evening of Sukkot. Sukkot is profoundly about beauty, and the *sukkah* that we build should reflect our best nature, so that it is in this spirit that we decorate it, as though it were the Jewish child's answer to the Christmas tree. It is also true to say that the *sukkah* represents the very transience of all endeavor. Sukkat teaches us that although we may live in a mansion, we might easily have to live in a hut the next day. We should rejoice in both these possibilities. The *sukkah* is also great fun for the children to sleep in, as a kind of joyful game and adventure.

Usually, people use the *sukkah* only as a place to eat. It is good to eat there at night, and recite kiddush over wine and the blessing of *motsi* for bread.

We need to rejoice in the *sukkah,* not suffer in it, there is therefore no need to sleep there in inclement weather.

MAKING YOUR OWN *SUKKAH*

Sukkot is the authors' family's favorite holiday. We have a semi-permanent frame in the yard with hooks built in for the walls of cloth. This makes constructing the sukkah very easy and allows us to dedicate most of our attention to the decoration. Our frame is made of wood, though PVC or metal pipes are an easy alternative. We hang painters' drop-cloths, made of canvas, on the inside, and blue plastic tarpaulins on the outside to protect the *sukkah* from wind and rain and keep it snug on chilly nights. We also hang all kinds of beautiful woven cloths, embroidered tablecloths, pretty bedsheets, and even some real tapestries. Sequined fabric for the interior walls is also wonderful, as it catches the sunlight.

Judith Hankin.

Etrog container, *Augsburg, 1670–80, made from silver, Jewish Museum, New York.*

We place rugs bought secondhand on the ground and many
pillows, cushions, and blankets. Some years we place a big tin pan
on the floor—which becomes our hearth—and burn a log at night
to keep us warm. The roof is made of branches festooned with all
sorts of sparkling things from the party shop and with paper
flower garlands. We also hang tiny holiday lights that provide the
illumination we need at night. It is magical.

During the evenings we always have friends over for potluck
dinners. During the day we read and play in the *sukkah*, and even
teach our students there. We always hate to see the holiday end
so that when we stop spending time in the yard, we move our
activities back into the house. It is wonderful to have a protected
room in the garden, but often the rains come during Sukkot.
Traditionally, if it rains while you are in the *sukkah*, you are to
return to the house and are not enjoined to return to the *sukkah*
when the rain stops; we are supposed to rejoice in the *sukkah* and
not endure discomfort there. In ancient times, Sukkot was called
Ha Hag, "The Festival" on which *ushpizin*—honorary guests—were
invited each night from the host of our holy ancestors. The *ushpizin*
are Abraham, Isaac, Miriam, Abigail, Moses, Aaron, David,
Sarah, Rachel, Rebecca, Leah, Esther, and so on, and we invite
two or three each evening to join us for dinner.

On the first night of Sukkot, we light candles in the *sukkah* and
recite:

> Blessed are you, Lord our God, Ruler of the Universe, who has sanctified us
> through His commandments, commanding us to kindle the festival lights.

Then we recite the *She-he-heyanu* blessing:

> Blessed are you, Lord our God, Ruler of the Universe, for keeping us in life,
> for sustaining us, and for helping us reach this moment.

If the candles look as though they will blow out, then someone
other than the person who lit them should carry them into the
house. Unlike the practice for Shabbat candlelighting, we first say
the *Berakhah* and then light the candles.

After evening services, or in general when you are ready to eat, the festival kiddush is recited over wine. Then the blessing for the *sukkah* is recited:

> *Praised are you, Lord our God, Ruler of the Universe, who has sanctified us through His commandments, commanding us to live in the sukkah.*

Traditionally we then wash our hands and follow this by Morzi over bread. By custom we should have two loaves.

THE FOUR SPECIES

The *Arbaah Minim* is another important mitzvah of Sukkot. It is also called the Four Species.

These Four Species are meant to show our connection with the land. The four species are *lulav* (palm branch), *aravot* (willows), *hadas* (myrtle), and *etrog* (citron). The choice of these has innumerable interpretations. Some teachers tell us they represent fire, air, water, and earth, others that they are four levels of reality. Another interpretation of the ritual that seems especially attractive sees the four species as symbolic of four types of Jews. The etrog has taste and fragrance and so represents Jews who have learning and a good nature. The palm tree has taste but not fragrance, like Jews who possess erudition but not good nature. The myrtle has fragrance and not taste, like Jews who possess a sweet nature but not erudition. The willow has neither. There are people who are neither good nor clever.

Each day of Sukkot there are special songs and chants, traditionally beginning with the words *Hosha na* (save us), reminding us of the symbolism of this holiday as a time of transience, as an understanding of the temporary nature of life, and the need to enjoy it.

The two most impor ant of the rituals are the circling of the synagogue seven times instead of once while carrying the four species and reciting the *hosha na* prayers, and the beating of the willows.

HOSPITALITY

Sukkot is a time for hospitality. In some communities people go from *sukkah* to *sukkah* "making kiddush"—that is, having at least wine and cake. Instead of a formal lunch at any one place, during the course of the afternoon they visit many *sukkot* in their neighborhoods.

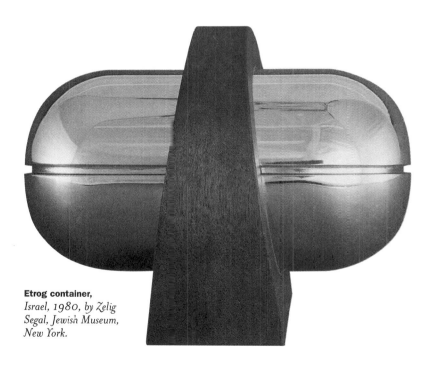

Etrog container,
Israel, 1980, by Zelig Segal, Jewish Museum, New York.

Recipe for Sukkot

As Sukkot is a harvest holiday, it is in keeping to look for a recipe that uses an abundance of vegetables and offers an overflowing platter. This recipe can be made as is, or modified for vegetarian palates. You can change the vegetables to suit your tastes. Do not be afraid of this dish. It takes a lot more time to gather the ingredients than to prepare. It is worth the effort. My husband, Fred, introduced me to couscous, after he had the good fortune to visit kosher restaurants in Marrakesh.

COUSCOUS
SERVES 10-12

1 ¹/₂ cups couscous, prepared by instructions of box
    (Prepare when ready to serve meal, so couscous remains hot)
1 cup chickpeas, drained
1 lb. carrots, peeled and halved, or use the same quantity of baby carrots
1 small cabbage, cored and sliced
1 tomato, cut up
1 turnip, sliced
2 sweet potatoes, cut into chunks
1 lb. leeks, cleaned and sliced into 1 inch portions.
    (Use white part only and save the greens for soup.)
2 large onions, quartered
2 zucchinis, sliced in chunks
1 small squash, of any variety, sliced
3 lb. chuck, flanken, or any appropriate cut
1 ¹/₂ chicken, in preferred cut
1 lb. Polish hot dogs
raisins, almonds or pine nuts (optional)
1 teaspoon coriander
1 teaspoon dill

1 teaspoon parsley
salt and pepper to taste
$1/4$ tablespoon each turmeric and ginger (optional)
$1/2$ tablespoon saffron
     (Soak in boiling water for 5 minutes before using, add total liquid mix.)
4 quarts boiling water, or to cover.

In a soup pot, put in all the vegetables, the spices and herbs, salt
and pepper, plus the meat and chicken. Reserve the hot dogs until
later, along with the tomato. zucchini, and squash. Bring to a
boil, reduce to simmer, and cook until done, approximately 2
hours, or until meat is tender. Remove all vegetables and meat
from the pot and add the ingredients that have been reserved.
Cook until tender.

To serve, use a large platter. Spoon the couscous onto the
platter. Top with the sliced or chunked meat and chicken. Add
sliced hot dogs. Surround with the vegetables. Sprinkle lightly
the stock, and serve the rest of the stock as a gravy. Sprinkle with
raisins and nuts, if desired.

This dish is often served with *harissa*, or hot sauce, and
spicy salads. The cucumber salad for Shabbat would be good with
this meal.

Glossary of Terms and Traditions of Interest

Aravah The willow tree, used in the Four Species ritual of the Sukkot. Its presence arises from the belief that it is shaped like the mouth and that because it has no taste and no smell, it represents those Jews who fail to do good deeds and who pay no attention to the Torah.

Chol Hamo'ed Intermediate Days of a festival. Days in the middle of a festival on which most ritual strictness is relaxed.

Etrog A citrus fruit of the hadar tree and one of the four species used in the Sukkot ritual. It is said to be shaped like the heart and therefore symbolizes Jews who have a knowledge of the Torah and do good deeds.

Hadas The myrtle, another of the four species used in the Sukkot ritual. It symbolizes the eye and represents Jews who do good deeds but do not read the Torah.

Hoshana Raba 7th day of Sukkot Shalosh Regalim—3 Pilgrimage Festivals. On Sukkot, Passover and Shavuot, Israelites journeyed to the Temple in Jerusalem.

Kohelet Book of Ecclesiastes read on the 8th day of Sukkot. "There is nothing new under the sun."

Lulav The palm, another of the four species items used in the Sukkot ritual, symbolizes the spine and represents those Jews who read the Torah but do not do good deeds.

S'chach The evergreen twigs used to make the roof of the sukkah. The important aspect of these twigs is that they enable the occupier to the hut to see the stars throught the roof.

Z'man Simchataynu Another name for the holiday, "Season of Our Joy."

Simchat Torah:
REJOICING WITH THE TORAH

Right after the last day of Sukkot follows the Simchat Torah, the Eighth Day of Assembly -TISHRI 22-23

> On the eighth day hold a solemn gathering and don't work at your occupations.
> -NUM. 29:35

God asks anyone who has made a pilgrimage for Sukkot to remain with Him/Her one extra day. The joyous character of Simchat Torah and its rituals at the ending and beginning of the Torah reading cycle has made it one of the most widely celebrated rituals of the Jewish festival cycle.

Traditions and Customs

SHEMINI ATZERET

Shemini Atzeret is a 'hag'—a full festival day. The usual rituals of kiddush, and candlelighting are observed and the requirement not to work. It is called *Shemini Hag ha'Atzeret* in the kiddush and the

63

Amidah. The *She-he-heyanu* blessing is spoken at candlelighting and/or at kiddush.

At the time of the *Musaf* service, we say the prayer for rain (*Tefillat Geshem*) for the first time. The transition to the prayer for dew is made at the beginning of Passover. Each of these prayers notes a change in the agricultural year in Israel, where it doesn't rain in summer. In this time the heavens are deciding how much rain we will have during the year. Though we may indicate our needs for water with rituals of the temple—water libation and the four species—we do not actually pray for rain until the end of our living outside in the *sukkah.* "Praise God who brings forth the winds and brings down the rain," we chant. Next to Purim, there is no holiday which generates more joyous abandon in dance and celebration than Simchat Torah.

The yearly reading of the Torah is concluded, and immediately begun again and rituals include *hakkafot* (circlings) similar to the *hoshana* ritual of Sukkot, which involves singing and dancing in honor of the Torah. Customarily there are seven *hakkafot* at night when we read the last section of Deuteronomy, the very last verses being read the next morning.

Megillah, *a parchment made up of four parts glued together with handwritten Hebrew text, from Germany. Judaica Collections of Max Berger, Vienna, Austria.*

In the evening we begin the celebration of Simchat Torah. Following the *Amidah*, the *hakkafot (circlings)* begins with the recital of songs in praise of God and the Torah. The congregation follows the leader and repeats each verse. On recital of the verse *Vayhi binsoa ha-aron* ("It came to pass whenever the ark …"), the ark is opened up, and the Torah scrolls are removed from the ark. (In some congregations the ark is never left empty—either a lighted candle or a Bible is left inside.) It is an honor to carry a Torah scroll during a *hakkafah,* and even more of an honor to lead the procession.

There are several people holding the Torahs and moving around the synagogue. The rest of the congregation kiss the Torah scrolls as they pass.

Following the procession the leader sings a song and the congregation joins in with the song and dances. The dancing can be spontaneous, and the different groups usually change continuously. When the leaders become tired from their dancing, they pass the Torah scrolls on to others.

Eventually the first *hakkafah* stops—there is no set time for this—and the Torah scrolls are passed on. The children are especially encouraged to participate, carrying flags, candles, and baby Torahs. There is more dancing with each *hakkafah,* and so on into the night.

Following the seventh and last *hakkafah,* all the Torahs except one are returned to the ark, and this one is used for the service. The Torah is usually read during the day but during Simchat Torah we read it at night. The Torah is often called a bride by tradition. Weddings are also often done at night, which is perhaps the origin of why we read it at night during this time.

The morning service is the same as any holiday, except there are again *hakkafot.* And during this holiday there are also many *Aliyot,* as everyone present must be honored with one.

When everyone has received an *Aliyah,* there follows a special calling up of the children named *Kol ha-Ne'arim*—"All the Children." A *tallit* is spread over their heads like a canopy and they accompany an adult in saying the blessings. This is intended to make them feel enclosed and secure beneath the wings of the adults.

The wedding imagery is continued during the day with bringing up *Aliyah* called "groom of the Torah." In the same way as with a Jewish wedding, the individual is sometimes pelted with candy and sweets. The Torah is

Mizrach *by Wolf Kurzman, 1903, Jewish Museum, New York.*

rolled back to the beginning, or a second one is brought. The *Aliyah* for the first reading is called "groom of Genesis." The entire congregation then recites *"v'hi erev, v'hi boker"*—"It was evening and it was morning...the first day." This is then repeated.

Simchat Torah is about the renewal of life—of love, the beginning of spiritual practice. The poet Shelley wrote, "When winter comes, can spring be far behind?" The end of the Torah comes; the end of teaching. In the very next breath, the Torah begins again. The spring is therefore symbolically reborn.

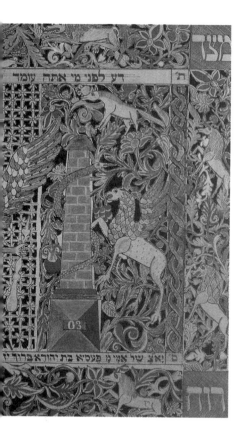

One important thing to be observed—Simchat Torah is intended to be crowded, so use a space that is a bit too small for everyone invited so that people can crowd in and be intimate and close, and so that the music is loud and strong to encourage an informal atmosphere, and one that is spiritually oriented and not heavily burdened with ritual.

Glossary of Terms and Traditions of Interest

Chatan Torah Bridegroom of the Torah—the one who blesses—reads the final section of Deuteronomy.

Chatan Beresheet Refers to the "Bridegroom of Genesis," the one who reads the first section of Genesis on Simchat Torah. It is considered a great honor to be asked to do this reading and blessing.

Degel A flag given to children, which they wave while taking part in the seven *hakkafot* of the Simchat Torah.

Hakkafot Circling dances with the Torah.

Maysheev ha-ruach u'moreed ha-gashem The most important phrase of the ritual of Praying for Rain, meaning "You who cause the wind to blow and the rain to fall."

Simchat Torah Means "Torah Joy."

Judith Hankin.

Hanukkah:

BRINGING LIGHT TO DARKNESS

The common version of the story of Hanukkah is well worth telling. In 167 B.C.E. King Antiochus Epiphanes forced Hellenization on all his subjects.

Jewish rituals were outlawed, and the worship of Greek gods replaced them in the Temple. Many resisted Hellenism and died as martyrs, though many also were forced into compliance, giving rise to the story that follows, and the rebellion which gave birth to one of the most famous legends.

The rebellion began in the village of Modi'in in central Israel. Here they forced local Jews to sacrifice a pig at the altar in order for them to show obedience to the new decree—a political move more than religious. Mattathias, an old priest, refused to obey, and, together with his five sons, began a rebellion. The war that followed was not one of fixed battles, but a war of attrition, ambush, and guerrilla tactics, and after the old priest Mattathias died, his son Judah took over the leadership of the rebellion, and eventually succeeded in defeating the Greeks. This great triumph of the very few against the many was the first miracle.

Finally, Judah freed Jerusalem and reclaimed the Temple, entering in after their triumph with no food or light and very little to sustain them at all. Once inside it, they found but one small

North African Hanukkah lamp,
Jewish Museum, New York.

container of oil, which was enough to burn for only one day. Upon lighting the temple menorah with it, a miracle occurred and the menorah burned for eight days. Hanukkah is therefore celebrated to recall the Maccabees and the conquering of the Greeks, but most of all to celebrate the miracle of the burning oil. This is the second miracle.

The First Book of Maccabees seems to have been written within fifty years of the re-dedication of the Temple. Hannukah is therefore the only holiday for which there are few historical records, as it is not mentioned in the Bible, though it is part of the apocryphal literature. The story of Hannukah happened after the Bible was redacted. In fact, the book of the Maccabees, while it emphasizes the war, makes no mention of the oil.

Hanukkah occurs over eight days not because of the miracle of the menorah remaining alight for that length of time but because it follows the timing of the holiday of Sukkot, which the Maccabees could not observe while they were in the mountains of Judea.

There is also very little in the Mishnah about Hanukkah. The miracle of the burning oil occurs only in later rabbinical literature. Because of the rabbis' discomfort with the emphasis on military victory, the miracle of the oil was given predominance.

In spite of this uncertain history, Hanukkah has become increasingly popular and the rabbis long ago made candlelighting rituals. These rituals emphasize the miracle of the oil, while relating the tale of the Maccabees.

Hanukkah has been influenced in America by Christmas. Hanukkah money, or *gelt*, given to children, is an old tradition, but the fact that Christmas is so close has made the exchange of gifts an important part of the holiday in most American Jewish families. Hanukkah is more important than the biblical holidays of Sukkot and Shavuot, which is a pity, since they are such important and rich holidays.

Traditions and Customs

LIGHTING HANUKKAH CANDLES

The most important ritual of Hanukkah is creating light. Hannukah continues for eight nights, and each night an additional candle is lit. This is the tradition celebrating and commemorating the eight nights that the burning oil continued. Most people use wax candles, though oil and wick may also be employed, as it is considered more appropriate for the accurate celebration of the original story where oil was used. It is customary to place the menorah in a

Seven-branched candelabrum *from Hungary, 1922, Jewish Museum, New York.*

window so that passersby can see the lights. The candles are placed in the menorah, starting at the right. Each subsequent night one candle is added, starting at the right and moving left.

There is a special place on the *hanukiah* for the *shamash* candle (helper), which is always lit first. Before lighting the candles, we say the following blessings:

Blessed are you, Force of the Universe, who has sanctified our lives through commandments, commanding us to kindle the Hanukkah lights.

Blessed are you, Force of the Universe, who performed miracles for our ancestors, in those days, in this season.

On the first night we recite *She-he-heyanu*
Blessed are you, Force of the Universe, for giving us life, for sustaining us, and for helping us to reach this moment.

The *shamash* is then used to light the candle. Every subsequent night, we begin by lighting the candle that has been added last. Once the lighting is completed, most people sing *Ma'oz tzur,* a beautiful song illustrating the protective power of a spiritual life.

After singing *Ma'oz tzur,* and other Hanukkah songs, gifts are given. And we play games, such as dreidel (*sevivan* in Hebrew).

To play this game, each player is given a stake—pennies, nuts, etc. A piece is put in the center to begin. The top or dreidel has four sides, each with a letter—*nun, gimmel, hay, or shin*—representing *nes, gadol, hay,* and *sham.* Players then take turns spinning the dreidel and following the instructions—the letter *nun* means neither win nor lose; *gimel* means the player can take the whole pot; *hay* means half the pot; *shin* means the player must put one coin in the pot.

Another custom at this time is to eat foods that have been fried in oil, such as potato *latkes* (Ashkenazim tradition) or *sufganiyof*—a type of doughnut (Sephardim tradition)—to remind us once again of the miracle of the oil.

Spinning tops *for traditional game at Hannukah, Jewish Museum, New York.*

Other Customs and Laws

Hanukkah lamp in the form of a Torah Ark
by Brody, 1787, Jewish Museum, New York.

Hannukah starts with one light and finishes with many. This is one of the great teachings of this holiday period. Transformation begins with the first step, one step at a time.

The only way to dispel darkness is not to curse the darkness, but to create light. Also, fire is dynamic. It must increase or shrink, and the very act of touching it spreads it further. The tiniest flame can ignite a bonfire. This is the teaching of Hannukah— the teaching of the Macabees. Let the heart become a bonfire.

So by the last day of the holiday, the candles or oil are burning most brightly—Zot Hannukah—the essence of Hannukah. The number seven is the perfect number in many mystical traditions, so that the number eight is beyond the complete, bringing something eternal. One step at a time to eternity.

KAVVANOT

Hanukkah is traditionally celebrated with are a number of traditional prayers and songs that are enjoyed following the candle-lighting. There are also other possibilities such as Psalm 70 and Psalm 44:2-9. We can also develop our own selection of pieces, such as the following from Michael Strassfeld's book, *The Jewish Holidays*. These can be read all in one night or divided among the eight nights.

On the first night:

The earth was unformed and void, with darkness over the surface of the deep ... God said, "Let there be light"; and there was light. God saw that the light was good, and God separated the light from the darkness. God called the light Day, and the darkness He called Night...

God said, "Let there be lights in the expanse of the sky to separate day from night; they shall serve as signs for the set times—the days and the years; and they shall serve as lights in the expanse of the sky to shine upon the earth." And it was so. God made the two great lights, the greater light to dominate the day and the lesser light to dominate the night, and the stars. And God set them in the expanse of the sky to shine upon the earth, to dominate the day and the night, and to separate light from darkness. And God saw that this was good.

—GEN. 1:2-5; 14-18

On the second night:

Woe to those who call evil good and good evil; who present darkness as light and light as darkness; who present bitter as sweet and sweet as bitter! Woe to those who are so wise—in their own opinion; so clever—in their own judgment!

Woe to those who are so heroic—as drinkers of wine, and so valiant—as mixers of drink!

Who vindicate him who is in the wrong in return for a bribe, and withhold vindication from him who is right.

Assuredly, as straw is consumed by a tongue of fire and hay shrivels as it burns, their stock shall become like rot, and their buds shall blow away like dust.

For they have rejected the instruction of the Lord of Hosts, spurned the word of the Holy One of Israel.

-ISA. 5:20-24

On the third night:

They have eyes, but cannot see; ears, but cannot hear.

They are rebels against the light; they are strangers to its ways, and do not stay in its path.

For darkness is morning to all of them; for they are friends with the terrors of darkness.

Indeed the light of the wicked fails; the flame of his fire does not shine. The light in his tent darkens; his lamp fails him.

They grope without light in the darkness; He makes them wander as if drunk. And I will banish them from the sound of mirth and gladness, the voice of bridegroom and bride, and the sound of the handmill and the light of the lamp.

All the lights that shine in the sky I will darken above you; and I will bring darkness upon your land—declares the Lord God.

Listen, you who are deaf; you blind ones; look up and see!

-PS. 115:5-6; JOB 24:13, 17; JOB 18:5~; 12:25;
JER. 25:10; EZEK. 32:8; ISA. 42:18

On the fourth night:

Thus said God the Lord, who created the heavens and stretched them out,
who spread out the earth and what it brings forth, who gave breath to the
people upon it and life to those who walk thereon:

I the Lord, in My grace, have summoned you, and I have taken you by the
hand. I created you, and appointed you a covenant-people, a light to the
nations—Opening eyes deprived of light, rescuing prisoners from confine-
ment, from the dungeon those who sit in darkness.

I form light and create darkness, I make peace and create woe. I the Lord
do all these things.

I will lead the blind by a road they did not know, and I will make them
walk by paths they never knew. I will turn darkness before them into light,
rough places into level ground. These are promises—I will keep them with-
out fail.

—ISA. 42:5-7; 45:7; 42:16

Judith Hankin.

On the fifth night:

Look at me, answer me, O Lord, my God! Give light to my eyes lest I sleep the sleep of death.

Darkness is not dark for You; night is as light as day; darkness and light are the same.

Now therefore, O our God, listen to the prayer of Your servant, and to his supplications, and cause Your face to shine upon Your sanctuary that is desolate, for the Lord's sake.

Send forth Your light and Your truth; they will lead me; they will bring me to Your holy mountain, to Your dwelling-place. With You is the fountain of life; by Your light do we see light. It is You who light my lamp; the Lord, my God, light up my darkness. The soul of a human is the lamp of the Lord, searching all the innermost parts. For You have saved me from death, my foot from stumbling, that I may walk before God in the light of life.

Truly, God does all these things, two, three times to a person, to bring him back from the Pit, that he may bask in the light of life.

–Ps. 13:4; 139:12; Dan. 9:17; Ps. 43:3; 36:10; 18:29;
Prov. 20:27; Ps. 56:14; Job 33:29-30

On the sixth night:

The Lord is my light and my help whom shall I fear! Bless the Lord, O my soul; O Lord, my God, You are very great; You are clothed in glory and majesty, wrapped in a robe of light; You spread the heavens like a tent cloth. Your word is a lamp to my feet, a light for my path.

The precepts of the Lord are just, rejoicing in His heart, the instruction of the Lord is lucid, giving light to my eyes.

For the commandment is a lamp, and the Torah is a light. Enlighten our eyes in Your Torah, attach our heart to Your commandments, unite our heart to love and revere Your name.

–Ps. 27:1; 104:1-2; 119:105; 19:9; Prov. 6:23; TRADITIONAL PRAYER BOOK

On the seventh night:

> *For the path of the righteous is as the light of dawn, that shines brighter and brighter until full day.*

> *Light is sown for the righteous, radiance for the upright. O you righteous, rejoice in the Lord and acclaim His holy name. The people that walked in darkness have seen a brilliant light; on those who dwelt in a land of gloom light has dawned. For all the Israelites enjoyed light in their dwellings.*

> *Arise, shine, for your light has dawned; the Presence of the Lord has shone upon you!*

> *O House of Jacob! Come, let us walk by the light of the Lord.*
>   –PROV. 4:18; PS. 97:11-12; ISA. G:I; EXOD. 10:23; ISA. 60:1; 2:5

On the eighth night:

> *Behold, there will come a time!*

> *And the light of the moon shall become like the light of the sun, and the light of the sun shall become sevenfold, like the light of the seven days, when the Lord binds up His people's wounds and heals the injuries it has suffered.*

> *In that day, there shall be neither sunlight nor cold moonlight but there shall be a continuous day, of neither day nor night, and there shall be light at evening time.*

> *No longer shall you need the sun for light by day nor the shining of the moon for radiance by night; for the Lord shall be your light everlasting, your God shall be your glory.*

> *Your sun shall set no more, your moon no more withdraw; for the Lord shall be a light to you forever.*

> *Cause a new light to shine upon Zion and soon may all of us be worthy to enjoy its light.*
>   –ISA. 30:26; ZECH. 14:6-7; ISA. 60:LG-ZO; TRADITIONAL PRAYER BOOK

Hanukkah greeting *card from Korea,*
Jewish Museum, New York.

Games and Festivities

Aside from the game of dreidel, which we play with the standard
rules, we can also play other, invented games such as a "spin-off,"
to see who can make the longest spin.

Another of the most ancient customs is storytelling. Whether
ancient or modern, the important aspect of storytelling is in the
telling itself. Many wonderful myths and fairy tales can be found
in any bookstore, and each person at the gathering can have a
turn in the telling on each of the eight nights. A book which
should be easy enough to find in the library or local book store,
containing many great stories is *The Chanuka Anthology.*

LIGHTING A FLAME IN THE TEMPLE OF THE HEART

Our homes are our temples, as are our bodies. During Hanukkah we rededicate our lives and our homes, our synagogues, to our freshened love of life and God.

For Sukkot we build a new "home," then in Hanukkah we bring new things to the home. And what is this new thing in the home? What are we trying to bring into our lives during this time? Fundamentally it's light that we bring, the light of compassion and affection. The basic intention of Hanukkah is to bring light, love, and concern into a world that often seems very dark. By doing this deliberately, consciously, for a period of time that is set aside for the task, we become hopefully more conscious ourselves, and every spark of consciousness produces more light.

After the long night of winter comes Hanukkah with its festival associations between light and dark.

Not by power, nor by might, but by my spirit, says the Lord.
—ZEKHARIAH 4:6

Lighting the menorah symbolizes lighting a flame of truth in our hearts. We put menorah in the window to show passersby that there is light in our temples and in our hearts.

Fundamental wisdom is not found through reading books, but by learning and absorbing the inner light. The light of the menorah is not for working by, but is a holy light to guide our souls.

Recipes for Hanukkah

LATKES FOR HANUKKAH
MAKES 8-10 PANCAKES   PAREVE

This is a variation on the traditional pancake, a little healthier and just as good.

4 large baking potatoes
1 large or 2 small zucchini
3 large grated carrots
1 tbsp. lemon juice
2 eggs
1 tbsp. sugar (optional)
2 or more tbsp. matzo meal
Kosher salt
Freshly ground pepper
Vegetable oil for frying

Finely grate the potatoes, either peeled or not, together with the onion. Sprinkle with lemon juice to keep the potatoes from turning brown. Put the mixture in a sieve and let it drain into a bowl, extracting the potato liquid. Reserve the sediment, which is potato starch. Grate the zucchini and the carrots. Put both mixtures into a bowl and add the eggs, matzo meal, and the potato starch. Mix well and season with salt and pepper.

Cook in a 12-inch skillet, adding oil to a depth of ¼ inch, until golden brown. (Work with 2 skillets at the same time if you want to make the recipe more quickly.) Drain the pancakes on paper towels, or brown paper bags. They may be kept in a preheated 300°F oven to keep warm. Add more oil to the pan as needed, preheating between batches.

Apple-Cranberry Sauce
Makes 8 cups Pareve

This sauce is great to serve with latkes, or as a side dish anytime.

3-4 pounds apples
   (cooking apples such as Rome work best, although any variety can be used)
1 bag fresh cranberries
   (raspberries would also be good—reduce sugar if using raspberries)
1 lemon
2 cinnamon sticks or 1 tbsp. cinnamon
1/2 cup liquid (this could be apple juice or water)
1/2 cup sweetener, more or less, to taste (honey, brown sugar, or white sugar)

The apples can be peeled or not. It is not necessary and the additional texture enhances the recipe. Core and quarter both the apples and the lemon. Cook in a heavy pot with the cinnamon and the liquid.

Cover, bring to a boil, and then simmer over a low heat. Add the cranberries when the apples start to get soft. If raspberries are used, add when apple mixture is almost ready. Stir frequently, so the fruit doesn't stick. If the fruit appears dry, add more liquid. Cook until the fruit is soft, about 20 minutes. Serve cold, or at room temperature.

Real Hanukkah Stories

RETOLD BY DANIEL LEV

When we think about Hanukkah what usually comes to mind?—
Eight days of candlelight, the miracle of the oil, the rededication
of our ancient Temple, and presents. Did you know that there are
two sources for the holiday of Hanukkah? There's not just one
story that explains it, there are two! Yep, one was the account
given by the Maccabee guerrilla fighters, and the other was passed
down to us from Chazal (the Talmudic rabbis). We usually mix
elements of each up into our present understanding of the whys
and wherefors of Hanukkah. So what are the stories?

The original account came down to us from the Maccabees
(whose name means "hammer"). They were involved in an anti-
colonial civil war against the Syrian-Greeks (known as the
Seleucids) and their Jewish allies (the Hellenists). First, a little
background: Around 326 B.C.E. Alexander the Great conquered
Israel. Alexander granted the Jews self-rule. Soon, Greek philosophy, art, and culture made its way to Israel and a number of Jews
began to assimilate into this new, exciting culture. After
Alexander died, his kingdom was divided between his generals,
with Seleucus acquiring the northern part of Israel and Lebanon.

About two hundred years after Alexander conquered the area
and promised freedom to our people, a set of evil Seleucid kings
began to take our freedom away. One of the last of them was
Antiochus IV, who made it a death penalty for Jews to practice
Kashrut (kosher laws), Shabbat, circumcision, or Torah study. They
also took over our Great Temple in Jerusalem and began celebrating pagan rituals in it, such as killing pigs. In addition, they
would send delegations of Seleucid soldiers and Hellenized Jews
to force us to practice paganism.

So here's where the Maccabees come in. One day a delegation
came into the sleepy farm town of Modi'in in central Israel. To
make a long story short, Matatiyahu, a farmer and Jewish priest,

Judith Hankin.

killed the invaders and along with his five sons began a guerrilla war against the Seleucids. Matatiyahu died soon after it began, and his son Judah continued leading the fight until the Jews won three years later. After they won back the Great Temple and cleaned it, they had an eight-day festival, one very much like Sukkot. "Then Judah, his brothers, and the whole congregation of Israel decreed that the rededication of the altar should be observed with joy and gladness at the same season each year, for eight days, beginning on the 25th of Kislev" (First Book of Maccabees).

And that's it! No miracle oil or menorah or nothing! Just a fun festival every year.

The second story, that of the Chazal (Talmudic rabbis), fills in the details we are already familiar with. Chazal, who came long after the Maccabees, were nonviolent and also did not support the corrupt, royal governments derived from the early Maccabees. They chose to ignore the militarism and new nationalism of Judah and his descendants, leaving us with a brief paragraph in the Talmud that summed up the spirit and practice of the holiday they wanted the people to observe. They wrote:

On the 25th day of Kislev, the eight days of Hanukkah begin. We are forbidden to fast and mourn for those days. When the Greeks entered the Temple, they defiled all the oils in it, and when the Hasmonean [Maccabean] dynasty prevailed over them and defeated them, they searched and found only one bottle of oil sealed by the High Priest.

*It contained only enough for one day's lighting. Yet, miracle was brought
about with it, and it burned for eight days..*
                                           —SHABBAT 21B

The text has us focus more on the light that illuminates the dark
places of our lives and further invites us to see the miracles all
about us.

Glossary of Terms and Traditions of Interest

Hanukkah Gelt A Yiddish term meaning Hanukkah money that is
used ot describe the coins or foil-covered chocolate coins given
each night of Hanukkah to children.

Hanukkiah The nine-branched menorah, used for candlelighting
and put in the window during the holiday celebration. Eight
branches stand for the days of the holiday and the ninth for the
servant of the house. It is used only for Hanukkah.

Latkes The Yiddish name for potato cakes, fried in oil and eaten
during Hanukkah.

Maccabee "Hammer" nickname given to the Hasmonean family
who lead the revolt.

Ma'oz Tzur The Hanukkah hymn "Rock of Ages," sung at home
and in the synagogue after the candlelighting.

Sevivon Hebrew for dreidel—top used on chanuka with four
letters signifying "a great miracle happened there."

Shamash The ninth candle in the menorah, representing the
servant; used to light all the other eight candles.

Sufganiyot A special doughnut filled with jelly and made originally
in Israel, eaten during Hanukkah because it is cooked in oil and
symbolizes therefore the miracle of Hanukkah, when the oil lasted
the full eight days of the first festival of Hanukkah.

Shonna Husbands-Hankin.

Tu Bi-Shevat:

JOYOUS PLANTING—A CELEBRATION OF TREES

Tu Bi-Shevat—the fifteenth day of the month of Shevat—is the New Year of the Trees. Originally a day which began as a tying of the ancient agricultural Israel to tithing—a time marked for tax payments—it developed into a period of planting and the first blossoms upon the trees. It has, in recent times, become a time to enhance our ecological awareness of the environment.

FROM THE KABBALAH

The Kabbalists have a saying: "As above, so below," which means that everything in the day-to-day world is a perfect mirror, or hologram, of the most mystical. We can also say that every aspect of the physical world mirrors the divine, and trees, in this context, are seen as mirrors of humans in their ideal form.

Here is a blessing for when we see the first blossoming tree of the year:

Praised are You, Lord our God, Ruler of the Universe, who has withheld nothing from this world and has created beautiful creatures and beautiful trees in it, so that people may delight in them.

Traditions and Customs

Tu Bi-Shevat Seder

The ritual of the seder involves eating fruit in order to help add freshness and purity, and all the blessings of this natural food back into the world through humanity. It involves eating ten different kinds of fruit in three different groupings, plus four kinds of wine. The number ten reflects the ten *sefirot*, and the different groupings of fruit are related to different levels of creation—four in all—*atzilut* (emanation), *beriah* (creation), *yetsirah* (formation), and *assiyah* (action or physical reality).

These are represented as follows:

1. **Atzilut** refers to spiritual creation that has no solid representation or symbol

2. **Beriah** includes ten different fruits, which are edible—figs, grapes, citrus, lemons, apples, pears, carobs, raspberries, quince, blueberries.

3. **Yetsirah** includes fruits that create pips but no shell, so they can be eaten; contain ten more varieties—olives, cherries, dates, jujubes, apricots, peaches, plums, persimmons, loquats, and hackberries.

4. **Assiyah** includes fruit (and nuts) having a shell that must be peeled and thrown: walnuts, pine nuts, pomegranates, pecans, coconuts, Brazil nuts, hazelnuts, chestnuts, and almonds.

The symbolism involved in these creative worlds is simple enough: the parts that are edible represent holiness; the inedible parts represent the impure; and the shells are a protection for the fragile inner divinity.

Shonna Husbands–Hankin.

A combination of the four levels of fruits is eaten with different wines, some white and some red, and sometimes red mixed with white. The wine is drunk only at the end of each session of eating the fruit.

During this period we symbolically return to the Garden of Eden. We look for harmony with nature as in the Garden. We avoid anger and bitterness. During Tu Bi-Shevat we reconnect to that symbiotic potential and the Tree of the Garden of Eden.

Glossary of Terms and Traditions of Interest

Ayz Chayim Means the "Tree of Life," and represents the Torah as a tree the faithful may hold onto.

Charuv The carob fruit, which symbolizes humility; it was much used in early times because it does not rot as quickly as other fruits.

Keren Kemet L'Yisrael Jewish National fund. In one century J.N.F. has planted more that 150 million trees in Israel, rehabilitating swamps and deserts, much of it through donations from school children.

Neti'ah shel simchah "Joyous planting" or "marriage trees'; a part of the ritual and custom of planting trees as part of various celebrations. The birth of a boy would bring the planting of a cedar tree, while a girl would cause the planting of a cyprus.

Shakayd The almond from the tree that is the first to blossom for spring. By the fifteeth of Shevat the almond tree in Israel is in full bloom.

Tapuach The apple, which symbolizes spring love and the glory of nature.

T'aynah The fig, which symbolizes peach.

Purim groggers (rattlers) *for making noise during Purim rituals to drown out the name of the Jewish arch-enemy. Hechal Shalom Wolfgang Museum, Israel.*

Purim:
BREAKING THE BARRIERS

Purim is the most raucously observed of all Jewish festivals. It is the last holiday of the biblical calendar, and its significance lies not only in the recounting of triumph over near tragedy, but in the story of the Jews living in non-Jewish societies.

Purim celebrates the ultimate redemption of good over evil, based on a story 2,500 years old. The characters are Esther, a quiet, young Jewish girl; a Persian King called Ahasueros, whom Esther eventually marries; Mordechai, her uncle; Vashti, the King's first wife; and Haman, the villain.

Queen Vashti defied the King and was banished from the kingdom. The King, by nature rather shallow, held a beauty contest, and chose Esther as the winner. Haman was appointed Grand Vizier, and Mordechai, for political and religious reasons, refused to support him. For this reason, Haman takes revenge on all Jews in the kingdom with a plot to kill them. He manages to persuade the King to sign a declaration permitting him to fulfill his vengeful plan.

Esther, however, discovers the plot and at the risk of her own life intercedes with the King during a banquet. She tells him that she's Jewish and condemns Haman. The King executes Haman and the Jews are victorious. The word "Purim" means lots or dice, in commemoration of the fact that Haman used lots to decide the day on which the Jews would be killed.

Traditions and Customs

We read the handwritten scroll that tells the story of Mordechai and Esther. Purim starts at sundown of Adar 14. Three blessings are said before the reading and one after:

Blessed are You, Source of the Universe, who has sanctified our lives through His commandments, commanding us to read the scroll [of Esther].

Blessed are You, Source of the Universe, who performed miracles for our ancestors, in those days, in this season.

Blessed are You, Source of the Universe, for giving us life, for sustaining us, and for helping us to reach this moment.

Then after the *Megillah:*

Blessed are You, Source of the Universe, who has championed our cause and passed judgment on our behalf. Praised are You, who saves the people from all enemies, for You are redemption.

Purim grogger (noisemaker),
Jewish Museum, New York.

When we read the story, each time Haman's name is mentioned, everyone drowns it out with loud noises from graggers, instruments, booing, and stamping of feet. Some may write the name of Haman on the bottom of the shoes with chalk so as to stamp it out with the constant movement during the service. Purim ends with a feast, or *sendah*.

Under Jewish law work is permitted on Purim, but generally we use the day for entertainment and festivities. One charming custom during this festival is to leave gifts of food for neighbors and friends called *mishloah manot*. Ideally these are left anonymously. Another custom is the giving of charity, and righteous generosity to the poor.

PURIM STICKPUPPETS

BY YEHUDIT STEINBERG-CAUDILL

Purim is a playful, fun, and creative time for celebration within the Jewish Yearly Cycle. It is a time to activate our imaginations, to create plays, puppet shows, costumes, and masks. One of the projects the children enjoy is producing a cast of characters in the form of stick puppets.

I have included some character faces that you can Xerox or trace. Be creative in the way you choose to color these with markers, puffy paints, and crayons. Then open up your scrap box, and add trims of lace, ric rac, or whatever your imagination leads you to—glue glitter, beads, sparkles, feathers...Your imagination is the limit to the ways you can decorate these faces.

Cut out the decorated face. Cut a 3-inch x 6-inch piece of gold, silver, or colored craft foil (purchased at your local craft store). Fold in half lengthwise, so that you now have a 3-inch square. Place a straw inside the folded foil in the center. Staple the straw and foil together. Glue the face onto the front of foil and continue to decorate with sequins, ric rac, and stickers. Allow your wild, playful imagination to guide you.

Finally, create a puppet show and enact the play for your family and friends. Write a script, create a little puppet theater. The possibilities are endless.

Recipe for Purim

FILO DOUGH HAMANSTASCHEN
PAREVE OR DAIRY

Lots of hamanstaschen—you are limited only by the amount of filling you use. One box of filo dough, available in most grocery freezers, makes a great deal of pastry. You can keep unused filo dough if well wrapped and stored in the refrigerator.

Use any traditional fillings with filo dough, instead of traditional pastry, for a different hamanstaschen.

Follow directions of filo dough. Remember to keep the dough covered and only work with one sheet at a time.

½ lb. clarified butter or margarine

> *(Clarify butter by heating in saucepan. When melted, remove from heat and let sit for 1/2 hour. Remove foam and put clear butter into a container. discard the whey—the sediment at the bottom.*

¼ cup vegetable oil
1 pound ground nuts—use almonds, pecans, walnuts, or pine nuts
Hamantaschen filling of your choice

Heat the oil, margarine, or butter together until melted in saucepan over low heat. Cut filo into 2 inch stripes with scissors. Work on top of waxed paper placed on a damp towel. Using pastry brush, brush strip with butter and sprinkle with nuts. Place a spoon full of filling 1 inch from short end of each strip. Fold up the strip like a flag, using all the strip. It should look like a triangle.

Put the hamentashen on a buttered baking dish, separated, and brush them with butter mixture. Bake at 350°F for 15-20 minutes, until brown. Remove from oven and spoon syrup mixture or jelly mixture over hamataschen.

Syrup mixture:

1 cup sugar
2 tbsp. lemon juice
2 tbsp. honey
½ cup water

Cook in heavy saucepan at a boil for 5 minutes.
Stir until sugar dissolves.

Jelly Mixture:

Use one jar of your favorite jelly with ½ cup water.
Heat in saucepan until dissolved.

Purim cup from Augsburg, 1965. *Jewish Museum, New York.*

Purim Story

RETOLD BY DANIEL LEV

Purim is magic! It isn't just a dress-up holiday for young children, it's a day of wonders and ecstatic joy for everyone. On Purim there is a moment in the Jewish year during which we can go beyond the science-based reality we so closely cling to. On Purim anything can happen: miracles, sudden good fortune...Magic! This is what the eighteenth-century Chassidim (spiritual followers) of the Reb Arieh Leib, the Shpola Zeyde, saw one Purim.

It happened that a Chassid came to the Shpola Zeyde and told him his problem: a wicked ex-Poritz (landlord) in the far city of Koznitz had accused him of stealing a chest of jewels. The Chassid said that the jewels were an inheritance from his recently deceased father and that the Poritz had hired two friends to act as "witnesses" against him. They were going to take him to court both to claim the jewels and send the Chassid to jail. The Zeyde told the Chassid to get the trial postponed until Purim day. "But Rabbi, who will be my lawyer?" asked the Chassid. The Zeyde told him not to worry, a lawyer would come.

The day of Purim arrived in the town of Shpola. It is traditional on Purim day to do all kinds of wild, fun-filled activities. One custom is to appoint people to act as a Purim-rabbi, Purim-police, Purim-doctor, and so forth. This Purim was special: the Zeyde ordered the community to put on a great Purim-trial to parallel the one that would go on in Kosnitz. Everyone gathered excitedly for the trial as the Purim-judge called the court to order, using a well-cooked chicken leg as a gavel. The Purim-bailiff quietly brushed the pieces of chicken skin off his shoulder and called the evil Purim-witnesses to testify. They presented their case while the Purim-bystanders threw popcorn at them. Eventually the Zeyde entered, dressed in a grand, white, three-cornered hat, red gloves, and a black eyemask. As the Purim-defense attorney, he brilliantly demonstrated the illogic of the

101

accusers' arguments and exposed their evil plot. The Purim-jury declared the Purim-defendant "not guilty" and the Purim-Portiz and his evil companions were thrown into the Purim-jail until it was time for the community *seudah* (festive meal). In the middle of the joyous celebration a telegram arrived from Kosnitz, informing the rabbi and all present that the Chassid was acquitted of all charges.

Purim painting *showing a Hasidic rabbi (right) with a Sephardic rabbi (left), and two Hasidim, from Safed, Israel. Isaac Einhorn Collections, Tel Aviv, Israel.*

The next day, the Chassid returned to Shpola and told the residents the story. He said that throughout the first half of the trial he was very nervous because the lawyer the Zeyde had promised had not shown up. However, just before be was going to have to try to defend himself, a stately looking man arrived dressed in a "grand, white, three-cornered hat, with red gloves and a black eyemask." The man introduced himself to the judge as the defense attorney and proceeded to tear the prosecution apart with his crystal-clear oratory. In the end, he, the Chassid, was acquitted, and the Poritz and company ended up being charged with fraud and perjury.

Glossary of Terms and Traditions of Interest

Hamanstaschen A German name for "poppy-seed pockets"—triangular-shaped pockets made from dough and filled with poppy seeds and cheese or fruits. The triangular shape symbolizes the hat or ear of the evil Haman in the mythological story of Esther and Mordecai.

Masechot The mask worn during celebration masquerades.

Matanot l'evyonim The gifts to the needy made during the holidays, usually consisting of baskets of food and fruit.

Pur In the story of Esther and Mordecai, the lots cast to determine the day on which the Jews would be killed.

Ra'asham The noisemaker, often a rattle, that is employed during the telling of the story of Esther and Mordecai whenever Haman's name is mentioned and that drowns out his name.

Seudah A festive meal at the end of Purim.

Pesah:
REBIRTH AND LIBERATION

Passover (Pesah) celebrates the Exodus of the Israelites from
Egypt. It begins on the fifteenth of Nisan and continues for
eight days.

Pesah, the feast of unleavened bread, is the oldest Jewish festival and begins the yearly calendar. The departure of Israel from
Egypt, from slavery to freedom, is the defining moment in Jewish
history. The holiday has also other names, such as *Hag Aa-aviv*, the
spring holiday which follows winter with new life, and *Zeman
heiruteinu*, which means the season of liberation.

Pesah is the time of hope and new life, and even as we meditate on our narrow lives and our history, we vow never to make
others slaves as we were.

After the Pharaoh's refusal to free the Israelites, God brought
the plagues, ending with the killing of the first born. The angel of
death passed over the houses of the Israelites, granting them leave
to hurry away with no time for the bread to rise. This unleavened
bread, *matzah*, is the symbol of the Jewish liberation.

The plagues and the parting of the Red Sea helped establish a
relationship between God and all Israelites, not only Moses. Each
event was of such magnitude as to create a trust and belief in their
God as the all-powerful divinity. Even as the Israelites hurriedly

Passover Feast, Russia. *Judaic Collection of Max Berger, Vienna, Austria.*

ate their last meal as slaves—dictated by God to be paschal lamb and *matzah*—the angel of death killed every first born of Egypt, passing over the marked doorways of the Israelites. God dictated that this day be observed in all ages, understood as a personal liberation, that all leaven be removed from the home and only unleavened bread, *matzah*, be eaten.

In addition, no work is to be undertaken on this holy first, second, seventh and eighth days.

During Passover *hametz* (normal risen bread) is to be disposed of, even the crumbs cleaned out systematically. Ovens and surfaces are cleaned and thoroughly investigated to make sure nothing leaven remains.

On the first two nights of Passover, there are seders—traditional feasts, during which the story of Passover is recounted. The book from which the story is recounted is called the *Haggadah,* which means literally "the telling." Four glasses of wine are drunk during the seder, and there are also rituals of eating *matzah,* bitter herbs, Hillel's sandwich, and *afikomen.* All this, especially the recounting of the story of Passover, is the essential part of the ritual and the tradition of this important holiday.

One of the new customs that seems to be becoming fashionable is the seventh night seder, also known as the freedom seder. This has developed into a freer form of the tradition, and can include alongside the Passover story any number of different stories that the participants wish to add as reflections of the states of enslavement which might be similar to that of Passover in other cultures or nations.

Nevertheless, whether following the old traditions or bringing new rituals to light, the process of this meal is to commemorate personal and social freedom throughout the world.

Ceramic Passover plate
on brass stand from Italy.
Jewish Museum, New York.

REMOVING HAMETZ

Preparing the house for Passover is a ritual in itself. We do not simply clean the dwelling as in any normal week. We clean it as part of the Passover rituals.

First we must completely clean the house, a deep cleaning of all surfaces, which are then covered to make a new surface. Then, we put all the year-round dishes and pots away in cupboards. The refrigerator and oven are both thoroughly washed and cleaned out. All food for the holiday (except fruits and vegetables) is considered special for just this holiday, and must be purchased as such prior to the holiday and kept especially for the holiday period. Some families "sell" the unleavened bread still in their possession.

SHOPPING FOR PASSOVER

European Jews generally do not eat the following foods during Passover: peas, beans, rice, lentils, sesame and sunflower seeds, millet, corn, and peanuts. Foods such as baking powder, baking soda, vinegar, and most liquors are made from grain and are not kosher for Passover.

Household products such as plastic wrap, aluminum foil, cleaning powder, detergents, and metal polishes require no supervision.

On the day before Passover—*Erev Pesah*—the eve of Passover—we ritually dispose of the last of our leavened products.

Finally we do a last search of the house, and read a blessing:

Blessed are You, Source of the Universe, who has sanctic-
fied us through commandments, commanding us to
remove all hametz.

In our own home we hide ten pieces of
leaven (and make a list so that we
don't lose track of where they are!).
The children search for them
with a large wooden spoon,
a candle, and a feather
(to sweep the *hametz* into
the spoon). When all
is gathered we take
it into the yard
and burn it.

Seder towel *from Frankfurt.*
Made of linen and embroidered
with silk crochet.
Jewish Museum, New York.

108

After this ritual has been completed we say:

> All leaven in my possession which I have not seen or removed or of which I
> am unaware is hereby nullified and ownerless as the dust of the earth

This formula is recited again next morning, and once again, after the burning of the remaining *hametz*. For the latter event, some might also recite the following *kavvanah* (meditation):

> Our God and God of our ancestors, just as I have removed all hametz
> from my home and from my ownership, so may it be Your will that I merit
> the removal of the evil inclination from my heart.

THE SEDER TABLE

The seder table should be as beautiful as we can make it. We use the best china, crystal, and the best cutlery we have. If at all possible the plates and glasses should be kept for the exclusive use at the seder table during Passover.

The seder plate—*k'arrah*—contains all the symbols of the seder. These foods, which are not eaten during the seder, include:

1. **Karpas** A green vegetable such as parsley. This symbolizes spring and rebirth and is dipped in salt water near the beginning of the seder.

2. **Maror** Bitter herbs. Either romaine lettuce or horseradish is used as a symbol of the bitterness of slavery.

3. **Haroset** A mixture of chopped apples, nuts, wine, and spices or other recipes. The maror is dipped into haroset to reduce the bitter herbs' taste.

4. **Z'roa** A roasted bone, commonly a shank bone, which acts as a symbol of the Passover sacrifice. Vegetarians sometimes use a pascal yam.

5. **Beitzah** A roasted egg, symbol of the festival sacrifice.

THE WINE FOR PASSOVER

Kosher wine or grape juice is needed for the ritual of the Four Cups. Every person at the seder must drink four cups—arba kosot —of wine. For those who do not want to fall asleep or those who cannot drink wine, grape juice is normally substituted.

TRADITIONAL WORDS AND ORDER OF THE SEDER

1. Over the first cup of wine, we recite kiddush (to sanctify the day). Traditionally, before a meal we wash our hands and recite a blessing. For the *Urhatz* ritual we wash our hands but do not recite a blessing.
2. We dip a vegetable, as a symbol of renewal, into the salt water. The salt water symbolizes the tears shed by the slaves in Egypt.
3. We take the middle of three *matzot* and break it in half. We wrap the bigger piece (called the *afikomen*) in a napkin and put it aside to be eaten at the end of the meal, after being hidden and found by the children. The smaller piece is put back between the other two *matzot*. This act symbolizes the poverty of slavery.
4. We recite the words, "This is the bread of affliction that our ancestors ate in Egypt."
5. "This year we are slaves, next year we will be free."
6. The next part is usually recited by the youngest child present: "Why is this night different?"
7. The answer comes—"We were slaves to Pharoah..." The Four Questions, are never directly answered in the *Haggadah* but involve the telling of the story itself. There also occurs here a recitation of the ten plagues.
8. Next we point to the *matzah* and *maror*.
9. We say, "In each generation, every individual should feel personally redeemed."
10. "Therefore, since God redeemed us, we must glorify the Holy One and sing praise."

11. A final blessing concerns ultimate redemption and hope for the future. Then we take the second glass of wine.
12. We wash our hands and recite a blessing.
13. Three matzot are taken and two blessings recited—a regular blessing for bread and a special one for *matzah*.
14. Next the bitter herbs are dipped in a *haroset*, and the blessing for *maror* is spoken.
15. We then take the bottom *matzah* and make a sandwich of the *maror*, called a *Hillel* sandwich.
16. Finally, the festive meal is eaten.

Seder plate.
Jewish Museum, New York.

17. The last act is the eating of the *afikomen*, which has now been ransomed from the children who found it. We keep a bit to eat and bless when we are in need throughout the year.
18. Grace is then said, and the blessing over the third cup of wine.
19. Songs follow now, and we celebrate our hopes for the future.
20. More psalms and the door is opened for Elijah. This is often done by a child. A cup is placed on the table for Elijah.
21. In conclusion, we chant "Next year in Jerusalem."
22. We sing "Chad Gadya" and other songs and drink the fourth cup.

Avram Davis.

Passover Recipes

GEFILTE FISH

20 SERVINGS PAREVE

This wonderful, easy to serve loaf can be served at Passover, or any Jewish holiday meal. Omit the eggs yolks for a lower cholesterol dish. I like my gefilte fish on the sweet side. If you don't, leave out the sugar.

Each loaf makes 10 slices. One slice, per person, is usually enough if this is part of a large holiday meal.

3 ½ pounds ground fish fillets
  (whitefish, pike, buffalo, lake trout, or any other combination you prefer—I use ½ whitefish. ¼ pike and finish off with buffalo, although lake trout is great, also)
3 large onions, chopped fine
3 ribs of celery, chopped fine
3 large carrots, peeled and grated
1 tbsp. salt
½ tbsp. ground white pepper
3 tbsp. sugar (optional)
¼ cup ice water
2 tbsp. canola oil
½ cup matzo meal
2 heaping tbsp. white horseradish
4 extra-large eggs, or 8 egg whites
½ cup snipped dill (additional for garnish)
2 sliced, cooked carrots, for garnish (optional)

Preheat oven to 350°F. Place the ground fish, onions, celery, carrots, salt, pepper, and dill (and sugar if desired) in a large bowl; stir to blend. Stir in the ice water and matzo meal. Separate the eggs, and beat the egg whites with an electric mixer until soft peaks form. Mix the yolks (if used) into the fish mixture, then add the fish mixture to the whites, gradually. (At this point you can test the seasonings by taking a small amount of the mixture, and cooking it thoroughly. Cool to taste it, and adjust the seasonings, if necessary.)

Coat 2 9x3–inch pans, using vegetable oil cooking spray and line the pans with wax paper or foil, spraying the lining. Spoon the mixture into the pans and smooth on top. Place the loaf pans in a larger pan.

Place in preheated oven and add 2 inches of hot water to larger pan. Cover pans with sprayed foil or wax paper. Bake for about one hour, remove pan from water, chill in the pans at least 6 hours, or overnight. Serve by removing loaf from pan. Place sliced loaf on platter or individual plates, garnished with additional dill and sliced carrots.

Note: I once tried to short circuit the steps and did not use the boiling water around the loaf pan. The fish was definitely dried, and did not have as fine a texture as when cooked in a water bath.

MARINATED ARTICHOKES

4-6 SERVINGS PAREVE

This is a Sephardic vegetable dish that makes the Passover meal interesting. Artichokes are my son Élan's favorite food.

2 9-ounce packages of frozen artichokes
     (Canned may be used if frozen are unavailable.
     You can use fresh, but you have to do a great deal more work.)
¼ cup lemon juice
2 tbsp. honey or sugar
2 tbsp. oil
½ finely minced sweet onion
¼ cup chopped parsley

Put frozen artichokes in a pot and cook in one quart of water that contains the honey or sugar, lemon juice, and oil. Cook for 10 minutes. Drain, and place in serving bowl. Add onion. Boil the cooking liquid until it is reduced in volume to about ½ cup. Pour over artichokes and serve at room temperature. Sprinkle with parsley.

Kiddush cup *for Passover, silver,*
from Nuremberg, Germany.
Jewish Museum, New York.

The Continuation and Conclusion of Passover

Synagogue services throughout the week include prayers and blessings for dew and good harvest through healthy rainfall. Songs and melodies vary each day and reflect how much our lives depend on the fall of rain.

The second seder of Passover contains a blessing that begins the *omer*—a specific measure of wheat brought for the Temple offering during Passover. Recitations include the following:

Praised are You, God, Ruler of the universe who has sanctified us through your commandments, commanding us to count the omer.

This continues through Shevuot blessing and naming the count of each day. The seventh day of Passover is a *yom tov*—a full festival day. This day celebrates the crossing of the Red Sea by the Israelites, and some people now follow the tradition of pouring water on the floor and singing and dancing to commemorate the story. Many observe an 8th day. Yizkor, the memorial service, is held on the last day. Many sephardic Jews conclude Passover with a gathering called *Maimuna*.

Seder plate, *made from silver, center showing the Star of David. Judaica Collection of Max Berger, Vienna, Austria.*

Glossary of Terms and Traditions of Interest

Afikoman The larger portion of the middle of the matzot that is put aside at the beginning of the seder plate and then eaten at the very end after a search by the children who must be bargained with to obtain it.

Arba kosot The four cups of wine that are served during the seder.

Arba kushiyot The four questions asked by the youngest child during the early part of the seder.

Baytzah A roasted egg that forms part of the seder dish.

Bedikat chamaytz The search for the leavened bread at the very end of the house cleaning before Passover. In order to make the search real, a few crumbs are left to be found, normally by the children of the house.

Chamaytz, or hamaytz The leavened or sour bread sold to a non-Jew before Passover and then bought back.

Charoset One of the foods of the symbolic seder plate, usually consisting of nuts, apples, cinnamon, and wine; symbolizes the mortar used by the Israelites that was used to put up the buildings for the Pharoah during the enslavement of the Jews.

Chazeret The bitter herbs used on the seder plate - any vegetable with a bitter taste, such as radish or watercress.

Elijah's cup Set for the prophet who visits each seder. He symbolizes hope for redemption.

Haggadah "Telling" book of Seder - stories and rituals.

K'arah The seder plate at Passover.

Karpas The green vegetable on the seder plate, usually parsley or lettuce or celery.

Koraych The sandwich made from the *maror* and *matzah* during the Passover meal.

Lechem oni The bread for the poor, and the third piece of the *matzah* on the seder plate.

Maror The bitter herb symbolizing the slavery of the Jews in Egypt—usually horseradish.

Matzah The unleavened bread permitted during Passover; made by not allowing bread to rise during the early stages of preparation.

Pesah Literally, "to pass over or skip past," as did the angel of death that killed the firstborn sons during the enslavement of the Jews in Egypt. "Passover" in English.

Rachatzah The washing of the hands during the ritual seder of Passover.

Seder The ritual meal of Passover, though the word actually refers to the order of the meal, divided into fifteen parts.

Tefillat Tal The prayer for rain or dew, recited at the *Musaf* service on the first day of Passover.

Z'roa The roasted shank bone on the seder plate, seen as a symbol of the hand of God stretching out to the Jews.

Counting the Omer:
COUNTDOWN TO SINAI

The *omer* begins on the second night of Passover and continues through Shavuot. *Omer*, refers to counting the measure of wheat or other grain brought ot the temple at Passover.

We are commanded by the Torah to count seven weeks.
From the day after the sabbath, the day that you bring the sheaf of wave offering, you shall keep count until seven full weeks have passed. Bring from your settlements two full loaves of bread as a wave-offering... On that same day you shall hold a celebration, it shall be a sacred occasion for you..

-LEV. 23:15-21

Why is it important to count the days from the bringing of the *omer* until Shavuot? Originally it was the beginning of the harvest, a very important, perhaps even the most important, aspect of the year, as it provided all the food for the community.

Shavuot, which is an agricultural festival marking the end of the harvest and receiving the Torah at Sinai. Shavuot means "weeks" and refers to the seven weeks in which the omer is counted. Until the *omer* was offered on Shavuot it was forbidden to eat of the new crop.

Today the Omer is a time of preparation. We are meditating and preparing ourselves for the receiving of Torah. What does it mean to you to receive torah? It is a profound time of introspection.

Customs

THE COUNTING

The days of counting are still part of the ritual between Passover and Shavuot, following a prescribed procedure.

First, while standing, we recite the following blessing:
Praised are You, Divine Source of the universe who has sanctified us with His commandments, commanding us to count the omer.

This is followed by the count for the day:
Today is the first day of the omer.

Weeks are also counted, for example:
Today is the seventeenth day of the omer, *which equals two weeks and three days of the* omer.

There is ample opportunity to feast and dance during the counting, and families come and light bonfires. Parents bring very young children to *halaka*—the cutting of hair for the first time.

HALLAH

One famous custom is to prepare *hallah* and make it in the shape of a key, then sprinkle it with sesame seeds as a traditional reminder of *manna*, which first fell during the month of Iyyar in the desert.

Shonna Husbands-Hankin

Holidays during Omer

YOM HA-SHOAH: *The Day of Remembrance of the Holocaust*

Yom ha-Shoah was established on April 12, 1951, by the Israel government to commemorate the unquantifiable loss of millions of people during the Holocaust. In Israel, all theaters and places of amusement, banks, schools, and most businesses are closed. Commemorative services are held all over the world. Because this holy day is still so new, the way in which it is practiced is still very fluid, and varies from community to community.

YOM HA-ATZMA'UT: *Israeli Independence Day*

The return of the Jewish people to their homeland has been celebrated since the year 1948—the date of the founding of the State of Israel. On this date everyone in Israel celebrates with gatherings, parties, dramas, and parades, as well as with a full set of rituals and liturgies. The traditions of Yom ha-Atzma'ut include candlelighting, visiting the graves of loved ones, and lighting torches.

Matazah Bag.
Jewish Museum, New York.

Sirens are sounded at the end of the day, heralding a period of silence. This is then followed by celebration and filled with rituals of joy.

In some ways this is a counterpoint to *Yom Ha-Shoah*. It is meant to be a day of joy and redemptive optimism.

YOM YERUSHALAYIM: *Jerusalem Day*

Yom Yerushalayim, which celebrates the capture of Jerusalem during the Six-Day War, falls on the twenty-eighth day of Iyyar.

LAG B'OMER

The 33rd day of the *Omer* is celebrated with picnics and bonfires. Traditionally it is a period of mourning and no marriages. A plague afflicting Rabbi Akiva's students ceased on this day causing rejoicing and a lifting of prohibitions.

CLOSE OF THE HOLIDAY

At the end of the *omer* period we celebrate Shavuot—the time of receiving the Torah. The first few days of Sivan are considered special. The first day is Rosh Hodesh, the minor holiday celebrating the beginning of each new month. The second of Sivan is known as Yom di-Miyuhas (the day of connection) because it connects Rosh Hodesh and the three days of preparation for Shavuot.

As the *omer* draws to a close, our steps lead us toward Sinai.

Shavuot:
RECEIVING THE TORAH

Shavuot, sometimes known as Pentecost, is a holiday to celebrate the receiving of the Torah on Mount Sinai. Shavuot began as an agricultural holiday, but by late biblical times it was embraced as a feast of the law. We say that on Shavuot we all heard the voice of God telling us how to live proper lives and how to be filled with his divine light.

Customs

A tradition that derives from the kabbalah is to stay up without sleep during the whole night of Shavuot and study the Torah. Staying up all night not only points towards thirst for wisdom, but mystically is believed to help create healing for all the world. Our own community undertakes a group *mikveh,* a ritual purifying immersion in the morning. Others decorate their homes and synagogues with fresh fruits, flowers, and green boughs and paper cuts.

It is also customary to eat sweet milk products (cheese blintzes, cheesecake) during this holiday, thereby symbolizing Israel, the land of flowing milk and honey. The Book of Ruth is read on Shavuot, and we recommend making this a custom in the home. Ruth is the beautiful story of a young woman who experiences many difficulties, both physically and emotionally, in order to follow her spiritual dictates, and the indications of her heart. The story is told against the backdrop of the harvest, and Ruth, who is a convert to the Jewish people, is the great-grandmother of King David, from whose line comes the Messiah.

The mystics also tell us that studying during the night may bring the opening of the heavens and the receiving of revelation.

The custom of confirmation, bringing the young to adulthood, is also celebrated at this time.

Shonna Husbands-Henkin.

Judith Hankin.

Recipe for Shavuot

SHAVUOT SOUFFLÉ

6-9 SERVINGS   DAIRY

As it is customary to offer dairy foods during Shavuot, here is a great dairy entrée. This dish can be made the day before. Bake before serving. My Mom likes me to make this when I visit Memphis. My Dad will eat anything I cook as long as it doesn't contain broccoli.

BATTER RECIPE

¹/₄ lb. butter or margarine, softened

¹/₄ cup sugar

6 egg whites, plus 2 eggs (reserve 2 of the yolks for the filling)

1 ¹/₂ cups low fat sour cream

¹/₂ cup orange juice

1 cup flour

2 teaspoons baking powder

FILLING

8 oz. package reduced-fat cream cheese

2 cups low-fat cottage cheese

2 egg yolks (reserved from batter recipe)

1 tbsp. sugar

1 teaspoon vanilla extract

Cook in preheated 350°F oven. Prepare a 13x9 baking dish. Using mixer, blend all ingredients for batter recipe together until well mixed. Pour half the batter into the pan which you have prepared with a coating of butter. Blend all the filling ingredients together with a mixer or in a food processor. Spoon filling over batter, spreading it smoothly. Top with remaining batter.

Bring to room temperature, if refrigerated. Bake for one hour, uncovered, until golden brown. Can be served with sour cream, jam, or fresh fruit.

Shavuot Story

Retold by Daniel Lev

I want to pass on to you Jewish teachings and stories that come from the deep, richness of our tribal tradition.

The holiday of Shavuot marks both a harvest celebration and the day on which we received the Torah, beginning with the first Ten Commandments, from God at Mount Sinai. Here I present a classic Midrash story that speaks to the secret of our continuity as a people.

At the foot of Mount Sinai, God gathered the elders of our people and said, "I'm willing to give you the Torah so that you may live the lives of Jews. However, you will need to provide me with those who will guarantee that you will keep this Torah." The elders discussed the matter and replied to God, "Our holy patriarchs and matriarchs, Abraham, Isaac, Jacob, Sarah, Rebecca, Rachel and Leah, will guarantee that we'll live a Jewish life." But God said, "Nope, not good enough." Oy vey! The elders went back to the Biblical drawing board and then replied, "Okay, God, how about our Holy prophets, like Moses, Isaiah, Devorah and Eliahu? Let them be our guarantors." God answered (you guessed it), "No way! They will not do as your guarantors." Finally, the elders bit upon a deep, insightful idea—they decided to consult with the elder holy women of the tribe. They then replied to God one last time, "Oh Holy One, let our children guarantee that we'll keep Your Torah." God said, "Good choice, I will accept your children as the guardians of the Torah."

Then God had all the children gather in one place at the foot of the mountain. All of the pregnant women were gathered as well, and God made their bellies as glass so that the babies within could be part of this great meeting. God asked them all, "Who is the One God?" In one voice they answered, "You are!" (The belly-babies answered, "bhu, bhu, bhu.") God then asked the children, "Will you make sure that this people will live as Jews according to the Torah and its later interpretations?" The kids said, "Yes!"

This midrash ends with a sad warning: when the adults neglect to listen to their children and they ignore the Torah, their children die as Jews, and forget who they are, I bless all of us that we listen to our children and co-create with them a Torah life we can all live by.

Glossary of Terms and Traditions of Interest

Chag ha-Bikurim The Festival of the First Fruits, which involves the taking of the ripe first fruits of the season to the Temple in Jerusalem as an offering. Seven "fruits" were permitted—barley, wheat, vines, figs, olives, honey, and pomegranates.

Chag ha-Katzir The Festival of the Harvest—the bringing of the two ceremonial first loaves of bread, which permits the community to eat the harvest.

Chag ha-Shavuot The Festival of Weeks, comprising the seven weeks counted from the second day of Passover until Shavuot.

Sefirat ha-Omer The counting of the *omer,* the measure of barley or wheat that was brought to the Temple on the first day of Passover as a thanksgiving offering.

Shavuot Literally, "weeks"—the Festival of Weeks.

Tisha Be-Av:

REDEMPTION THROUGH PAIN

Tisha Be-Av is a twenty-four hour fast, and commemorates the destruction of the first and second temples in Jerusalem, as well as numerous other catastrophes in Jewish history, such as the expulsion from Spain in 1492, Kristallnact during the Nazi era, Adam and Eve's loss of Eden, and the worship of the golden calf at Mount Sinai.

Tisha Be-Av, in the dark sense, marks epochal changes. We naturally prefer changes to occur through peaceful and loving means, but sometimes we must endure pain in order to achieve major changes, and this is the underlying aspect of this holiday.

Historically, this holiday marks the change from an agrarian temple-based culture to a more urban, sophisticated congregation culture. The entire theology of Judaism was altered in this transition.

Customs

During Tisha Be-Av, we take on the mantle of introspection in relation to the difficulties of our lives. There are therefore no weddings or other joyful occasions or celebrations, nor any

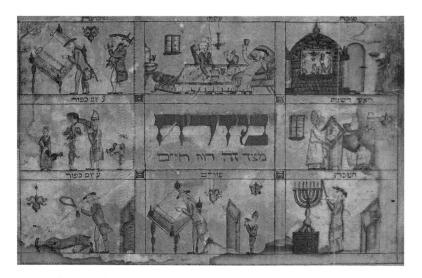

Mizrach, *decoration hung on walls at home to indicate the direction of prayer, facing east towards Jerusalem.*

gatherings where there is music. No food or wine except for Shabbat. No haircutting, shaving, swimming, or bathing is permitted. The fast begins at sundown and continues for twenty-four hours until the following sundown. The Book of Lamentations is read. No lovemaking, no wearing of leather clothes, and no use of oils or perfumes.

While many people do not wear shoes all day long on Tisha Be-Av, others refrain from doing so only during services. It is forbidden to exchange greetings on Tisha Be-Av, though you should respond if someone says hello to you.

However, as always within the Jewish celebrations, after a down comes a high. Though we are expected to experience the pain of life during this time, we are not expected to linger there, but to move forward into the rest of life from this place of understanding.

Tisha Be-Av Story

RETOLD BY DANIEL LEV

Beginning the ninth evening of the summertime Hebrew month of Av, Jews all over the world will mourn the loss of Jerusalem. Wait!—don't turn on the news to check for a distorted Middle East peace agreement or rifle through the newspaper to find the story of Israel's demise. Fortunately, for now, the modern State of Israel is intact and Jerusalem is her thriving capital. What we observe on the twenty-fourth is the historic destruction of both of our great Temples in Jerusalem. The first was destroyed by the Babylonians in 586 B.C.E. and the second by the Romans in 70 C.E. We call this day Tisha Be-Av, literally, the "'fifteenth of the month of Av," and, according to our ancient rabbis, it marks the day that these terrible events occurred. A number of other tragedies also occurred on this day:

1. the Hebrew spies sent into the land of Israel brought a bad report of the land, which led our tribe to doubt God, and this caused us to be con-demned to wander in the desert for forty years,

2. the British expulsion of the Jews in 1290; and

3. the Spanish expulsion of 1492.

On the day of Tisha Be-Av we abandon pleasurable experiences and practice a total fast (as on Yom Kippur). We read from the book of Lamentations in a mournful ceremony. We mourn not

Seder plate, *Vienna, 1900.*
Jewish Museum, New York.

only the physical losses that our people have endured but also the loss of our tribal and spiritual integrity that the ancient Temple represented. There is, however, a silver lining to this dark cloud of mourning: the rabbis said that on this day will be born the Messiah, the individual who will, with God's help, bring complete peace to the entire world and restore our people to wholeness. How, we may ask, can the messiah do this? The following story may begin to answer that question.

In a Christian country some centuries ago stood an ancient monastery that was famous for its inspiring church services, filled with hymns and glorious prayers. It made its livelihood through Sunday donations from the townspeople and sales of its wine and herbal products. However, over a period of some decades a very contentious lot of monks had joined the order who created a negative atmosphere in this hallowed monastery. They were selfish, suspicious, unforgiving, argumentative, envious, and at times would allow their evil characteristics to color their daily devotions, including the church services. After a while the people of the town stopped coming on Sundays, and the monastery began to experience a final decline. The Abbot, who was a good man, saw how his order was suffering but did not know what to do to revive the monastery's previous holiness and his monks' peace with one another.

One day, he found himself wandering in the nearby green woods pondering his predicament. At one point he raised his eyes and saw beside the road a small cabin. He didn't know exactly why, but he felt compelled to knock on its front door As he stepped up to the door and raised his hand, the door opened and a bearded man welcomed him in, bidding him to sit down to a cup of tea. "I'm so glad you arrive, Father. I have some great news to tell you. I am Rabbi Joseph, and during one of my meditations the Creator revealed to me that the Messiah is in hiding in your monastery and is living as a monk!" The Abbot was awestruck. He and the rabbi talked about the vision. Before the Abbot took his leave, the rabbi asked him to return later and report to him about his encounter with the Messiah.

Upon his return to the monastery, the Abbot announced to the monks that the Messiah was living among them as a monk. The brothers had great respect for the spiritual insight of their Abbot and believed him at once. Things began to change from that day. Each time a monk slighted another he quickly apologized, thinking that his brother may be "Him." Before long, the mood in the monastery changed and the few parishioners who still came to church spread the word that the services had regained their inspiration. Soon the church was packed for Sunday services and the monastery again became solvent. The Abbot was pleased with the changes, but he was also puzzled, because he could not discern which monk was the Messiah. He returned to his friend Rabbi Joseph to find out. "Where is the Messiah?" responded the Jewish master. "Why, look about you, my friend, in the renewed hearts and fellowship of your monks, in the eyes and joyous voices of your parishioners. There you will find the Messiah."

Glossary of Terms and Traditions of Interest

Avaylut Mourning time between the death of a loved one and the day of the funeral.

Bakashah The name given to one of the forms of fasting in Judaism, a request or plea from an individual or group in response to a time of misfortune.

Lamentations "Eicha" one of the books of Jewish holy writings traditionally read at this time.

Ta'anit tzibur Public fast.

Ta'anit yachid Private fast.

Tzom A fast.

Yerushalayim Jerusalem, meaning, "city of peace."

Charity Boxes.
Jewish Museum, New York.

PART II

Home Blessings

Megillah, *Austria, 1872.*
Judaica Collection, Max Berger.

The following is a story about blessing told by Zalman Schachter-Shalomi.

On Friday a Chassid came to Lublin to visit the Rebbe known as the Seer of Lublin for Shabbos. He came on Friday morning and went immediately to the Rebbe to announce his presence to partake of the Rebbe's greeting. The Rebbe, on his side, lifted up his eyes and looked at the Chassid.

"Please do me a favor," said the Seer. "Don't stay here."

The Chassid was shocked and disappointed. "Why not?" he asked. "I came all this way to see you. I traveled at great risk and great expense."

"Because," Reb Zalman quotes the Seer as having said, "I know you are going to die this Shabbos, and I don't want you to be around depressing everyone and bringing us down. Go to another village on the out-skirts of town. Stay in an inn, and you can die there."

On his way, the Chassid meets a wagonload of Chassidim on their way to the Seer. They tell him he's going in the wrong direc-tion and urge him to turn around. The distraught Chassid tells them his woe-ful tale.

"Don't be foolish," says one of the Chassidim in the wagon. "Why die by yourself

Shiviti, *a decorative prayer direction plaque set on a synagogue or home wall towards Jerusalem. The Jewish Museum, New York.*

in an inn where you don't know anybody? If you have to die this Shabbos, do it at the Rebbe's table. If you get sick and need help, we'll hold you up. Don't worry about a thing."

So, the Chassid got on the wagon and went back the other way, "By the way," said another of the Chassidim, "do you have any money with you? If you're going to die, you won't need it, and we can use a keg of schnapps to warm us on the way."

The Chassid shrugged his shoulders and turned over a 20-ruble note. On the way, Reb Zalman continues to recount, the Chassidim kept drinking and singing and saying, "L'Chaim," and giving their benefactor blessings for long life and good health.

When the Chassid arrived in Lublin, he once again returned to the Rebbe to announce himself. Once again the Seer looked up from behind his large eyebrows—"Wow! What a rebbe can't do for his Chassidim, his Chassidim can do for one another with their blessings and their L'Chaim!"

The Chassid lived a number of years more.

Shabbat

The only Jewish holiday that is observed every week during the entire year is Sabbath—the day of peace and rest. In the Ten Commandments, the only holiday that is mentioned as being imperative to keep is the Sabbath.

Remember the Sabbath Day to keep it holy.

Six days shall you labor, and do all your work.

But the seventh day is the Sabbath of the Devine, on it: you will not do any work, you, nor your son nor your daughter, your manservant, nor your maidservant, nor your cattle, nor the stranger within your gates.

A great Jewish legend tells the story of an Angel of the Sabbath who sits upon a special Throne of Glory, and on the Sabbath Day thousands of angels dance before this Sabbath Throne and sing in praise of the day of peace and rest, which, they say, is a foretaste of the World to Come, when all the people of the earth will live in everlasting peace, and every day will be as happy as the Sabbath.

Since a Jewish day is measured from sunset to sunset, the Sabbath starts on Friday evening. The house has been cleaned, and the table is set for the Sabbath meal.

Two *hallot,* known as *lechem mishneh* (double bread) are served to remind us of the Israelites, who gathered a double portion of *manna* on Friday to last for two days, because on the Sabbath they were not permitted to gather the food that descended to them from the skies —that is, *manna*. The cover on the hallot reminds us of the dew on the *manna* each morning and saves the challah's feelings as it is the last blessed.

As we light the candles we welcome in the Sabbath angels with three sweeps of the arms. The midrash says that each Jew has an extra angel reside with them on Shabbat.

The prayer is uttered:
> *Blessed are you, Divine Force of the Universe, Who has made*
> *us holy by Your Precepts, and commanded us to kindle the Sabbath lights.*

> *Baruch ata Adonai eloheinu melech ha-olam asher kidshanu b'mitzvotar*
> *v'tzivanu l'hadlik ner shel shabbat.*

The children are then blessed. For boys:
> *May the Holy One make you like Ephraim and Manasseh.*

Judith Hankin.

For a girl:

> *May the Holy One make you like Sarah, Rebekah, Rachel, and Leah.*

Then comes the priestly blessing for both:

> *God bless you and keep you, may God shine her face upon you,*
> *may God be cracious to you and give you peace.*

The Friday evening service (Kabbalat Shabbat) in the synagogue is short. L'cha Dodi is sung:

"Come, my friend, let us welcome Sabbath the Bride!" The blessing, Kiddush, over wine is recited in either the synagogue or at the home.

The Sabbath was a day of celebration and rest. Since the earliest times it is time to recoup and get in touch with those things that are truly important in your life. Think about it. If you cannot take one day off a week to dwell on the spiritual verities of life, then truly we, as a species are doomed. For there will never be a letup in the work of the world.

When our people were exiled to Babylonia after the destruction of the First Temple, the Sabbath took on a deeper meaning, for there we had no temple, and prayers took the place of sacrifices.

The laws and customs of the Sabbath are many. The Talmud devotes two volumes solely to the laws of Sabbath.

One story in the Talmud tells that when Moses went up to Mount Sanai, God said to him:

> *I have a precious gift, and I wish to*
> *give it to Israel.*

> *Is it the Ten Commandments? asked Moses.*

> *I shall give them the Ten Commandments, said God.*

Is it the Torah? Asked Moses.

No I shall give them that in due time, said God. This gift is even more precious. What can it be? Asked Moses.

It is the, said God. The Jewish people have kept the Sabbath and the Sabbath has kept the Jewish people.

Another story that tradition tells about the Sabbath involves a Roman governor who visited a great rabbi on that day. After the governor had eaten the food offered him, he commented on how good it tasted. The host told him that spice gave it flavor. The Roman wanted to order a quantity of the spice and asked its name. The host told him it was called Sabbath. Admitting he had never heard of such a spice, the Roman inquired where it could be picked. The rabbi answered that it did not grow but was actually a day of rest rather than a real spice. The Roman governor became a little suspicious and angry and asked the rabbi why this day of rest was different from any other, to which the rabbi answered with a question: "Why are you different from any other Roman?" The governor answered that he was different because the Emperor of all Rome had appointed him governor. So the rabbi said, "God was pleased with the seventh day and He appointed it the Sabbath."

For those caught up in the stresses of modern life, there is no greater tonic than keeping one day to rest completely.

The whole of the Sabbath Day is spent in happiness and relaxation. Sabbath meals are feasts, and they are accompanied by the singing of *Z'mirot*, which are special songs composed by rabbis and poets in different periods of our history in honor of the Day of Rest. These songs express the joy that is to be found in the Sabbath.

Spice container, *Venice, seventeenth-eighteenth century.*
Jewish Museum, New York.

After the meal Birkhat ha-Mazon, or Grace, is said, and then the family chats, entertains Sabbath guests, reads, or simply spends time together.

The morning of the Sabbath is taken up by services in the synagogue or walks in the woods or time alone with yourself or precious conversations of a deeper level with one's friends. If people go to synagogue there will be a torah reading and prayer. Then come another Sabbath meal, more Z'mirot, and the blessing after the food. Traditionally we eat three meals on Shabbat.

In general there are three daily services in the synagogue. Morning (Shaharit), late afternoon (Minhah), and evening (Ma'ariv). On Sabbaths, new moons, and festivals, there is a fourth, known as the additional (Musaf) service, which follows the reading from the Torah after Shaharit. The Kiddush (Sabbath and festival consecration of wine service), the Havdalah (ending Sabbath and beginning the week) and the Birkhat ha-Mazon (grace after meals) are outstanding examples of prayers for the home.

Among the most important daily synagogue prayers are the Shema (Deut. 6:4), which proclaims the unity and sovereignty of God; the Shmoneh Esre (or Amidah), consisting of eighteen basic benedictions that comprise the main portion of every service; the Ashre (Psalm 145); and the Alenu, which asks for unity of all under God's mantle.

Torah Readings

On Sabbaths, a *parsia*, or Torah portion is read either in the synagogue, in groups of friends, or by oneself. Congregants are honored by being called up to the reading. This act of going up is called an *Aliyah*.

Shonna Husbands-Hankin.

The section from the Prophets recited at the conclusion of the reading from the Torah is called the *Haftarah*, or "Conclusion." Each portion of the Torah has a specific *Haftarah* of the Torah has a specific *Haftarah* of its own, especially connected with it. Some Sabbath days are named after the *Haftarah* reading, such as Shabbat Hazon (Sabbath of Vision), when the first chapter of Isaiah (beginning with the words "The vision") is read. From the Talmud we learn that the practice of *Haftarah* readings on the Sabbath goes back to the first century C.E. when Jews could not read from the Torah itself upon threat of death by occupying

The Scroll of Esther *(detail)*, *Jewish Museum, New York.*

armies. Today, boys who are celebrating their Bar or Bat Mitzvah, and young people about to be married, are honored by being called up for the reading of the *Haftarah* or a special *Aliyah* to the Torah called an *auf-uf.*

In Israel Sabbath is special for most of the country shuts down. A spirit of peace and holiness descends upon the whole land. Offices, factories, stores, schools, theaters, are closed. Flower shops do their best business on Friday afternoons. Almost everyone brings home bouquets of flowers for Shabbat. The streets are quiet. Few if any cars. People walk with friends and family. Many people walk in the streets because of the peace.

In Mea Shearim ("One Hundred Gates"), an old, very Orthodox section of Jerusalem, men and boys dressed in long cloaks, or Kaftans, many with fur hats (streimlach) hurry to the

synagogue. There are many tiny synagogues in this quarter of Jerusalem. Each is frequented by a group of worshipers who have been praying together for many years. From these synagogues comes the chant of fervent praying. If we could look inside, we would see the worshippers swaying as they prayed, welcoming the Sabbath with all their hearts and all their souls.

Recipes for Shabbat

Recipes for Shabbat follow many traditions, but here are three side dishes that would be fun to add to any Shabbat table.

CUCUMBER SALAD

4-6 SERVINGS   PAREVE

Two peeled *cucumbers, very thinly sliced
1 bunch of green onions, cut in ¹/₄ inch pieces
2 tbsp. sugar
¹/₂ cup rice wine vinegar, or white wine vinegar
2 tbsp. kosher salt

Take sliced cucumbers and put in a sieve over a plate. Mix in salt and allow to drain. Rinse very well to remove salt. Put cucumbers in a bowl, add all other ingredients. Allow to chill for several hours, or overnight.

*If you use English cucumbers, they do not have to be peeled. If you want to make the dish more decorative, score the cucumber lengthwise, with a fork. If the cucumber has large seeds, the cucumber many be cut in half lengthwise and the seeds may be removed with a grapefruit spoon.

MOCK CHOPPED LIVER
4-6 APPETIZER PORTIONS   PAREVE

Even meat eaters enjoy this low cholesterol dish.

One can peas, drained
3 tbsp. canola oil
1 medium onion, chopped fine
2 hard-boiled eggs
Salt and pepper to taste
Sauté half of the minced onions. Process the peas, fried and raw
onions, and eggs in a food grinder or processor. Add salt and
pepper to taste. Refrigerate. Remove from refrigerator shortly
before serving.

POACHED PEARS
8-10 SERVINGS   PAREVE

This dish is easy to prepare and festive to serve. This recipe is
easy to double or triple, and is great for buffets. I would quarter
the pears if serving with other desserts.

6-8 pears
2 cinnamon sticks
3-4 whole cloves
$\frac{1}{2}$ cup sugar or honey
1 bottle grape juice or white wine (this is a great dish for leftover wine)

Slice pears in half or quarters, then core. Do not peel. Put in
an oven proof pan. Place cinnamon sticks and cloves where they
will be covered by liquid. Add sugar or honey and then the liquid.
Make sure sugar is dissolved. Cook in a 400°F oven, basting
occasionally. The pears are done when the liquid has turned into
a thick syrup. Serve at room temperature or chilled.

Shabbat Story

RETOLD BY DANIEL LEV

Shabbat, the Jewish day of rest, is most sacred to our tradition and provides us with a full-day, spiritual respite each week during which we celebrate, connect with our loved ones and the earth, and just "be" after a long week of "doing." To the Jews of Eastern Europe, the day was called *Shabbos,* due to the different Hebrew pronunciation they used. As Rabbi Abraham J. Heschel taught in his book, *The Sabbath,* our tradition tends to sanctify time and not materials. Shabbat is a prime example of our making time sacred. One way we do this is by refraining from work during the twenty-five hours of the Shabbat. The Talmudic rabbis even derived thirty-nine types of activities that comprise "work," all of which are forbidden on the Shabbat.

Reb David was faced with a predicament that shook him to the core of his Jewish soul. It began when David's Rebbe, his spiritual master, decided to move his community from Poland to a medium-sized city in Germany. Like a good Hasid (adherent of the path of loving-kindness), he and his family followed the Rebbe to Germany. It was the mid-nineteenth century and the industrial revolution was in full swing, creating a major challenge for Reb David. He brought his problem to the Rebbe.

"Rebbe, you know I was a cobbler in Poland and made a good living selling my shoes out of my little shop. But here I have no money to open up a shop and so I have to work in a shoe factory and they make us work on Shabbos! What can I do, Rebbe? I have to support my wife and seven children, but I also have to keep Shabbos."

The master stroked his beard for some time and then he gently soothed David with these words: "My sweet brother, you know that the commandment regarding Shabbos is written in two places in the Torah. However, there is a difference in the words used. In

עֵץ חַיִּים הִיא

Shonna Husbands-Hankin.

Exodus it says, 'Remember the Sabbath...' and in Deuteronomy it
says 'Observe the Sabbath..." So why did God use two different
words? This creates a logical problem. If we are to remember
Shabbat and keep it in mind, why do we need to observe it? And
if we are in the midst of observing the Shabbos practices, why
bother remembering? We can't do both at the same time. Perhaps
God wrote this because He knew that such a problem as yours
would arrive. Perhaps God knew that there would be times in a
Jew's life when he or she would not be able to observe Shabbos
completely. But in such a case do we just give up Shabbos? No!
When we cannot fully observe Shabbos, God gives us a way to stay
connected. God tells us we should *remember* Shabbos. So my dear
David, when you work in the factory on Shabbos, spend every
moment remembering Shabbos. Sing songs to yourself, review the

Torah portion in your head, recall previous Shabboses spent with your loved ones. If you do this, a most wonderful thing will happen to you."

The Rebbe took David in his arms and gave him a loving kiss and hug. David left to begin his new spiritual practice.

David did as the Rebbe suggested and soon he grew stronger and stronger in feeling Shabbos even in the midst of his assembly-line work. Then it happened that after some time he and his wife figured that they had accumulated enough savings to open up a little shoe store. They were elated: finally, David could come home for Shabbos and observe.

But something unusual happened on that first Shabbos. When David made kiddush, the table-wine blessing, he took a half hour to do so, and when he finished everyone felt bathed in the light of God. He likewise brought out the spiritual depths of the Sabbath during the singing, stories, teachings, and prayers he lead. It was even "worse" the next day when he came to the synagogue. Even the Rebbe was a little surprised at the light coming from David and the insightful teachings he shared with others.

After the services, he came to the Rebbe and said, "Rebbe, I don't understand what's happening to me."

The master put his arms on David's shoulders and softly answered his question: "My boy, you have followed my counsel well and spent every moment of your compulsory work on Shabbos remembering the holiness of this day. You have caused it to permeate your very being. My holy brother, you have accomplished what many desire—you are not just observing or remembering Shabbos, you have become Shabbos."

Shabbat Candlemaking

BY YEHUDIT STEINBERG-CAUDILL

One of the most effective family ritual-making projects is to make your own beeswax candles for Shabbat. This is a simple, easy and fun project, that can be done as part of the preparation for Shabbat the Friday before. It is appropriate for both children and adults. In fact, during Community Retreats, it makes a great children's activity, allowing them to feel included in the community preparation and ceremony.

Purchase a strip of beeswax from a local craft store. Cut it into 3-inch squares. Warm the wax squares between your hands for a couple of minutes. For each candle, proceed as follows:

Lay the warmed wax square flat on the table. Place a piece of paper under the wax, to prevent lint from attaching to the wax. Place a 3¼-inch length of wick on one side of the wax making sure to leave ¼-inch of wick extended beyond wax in order to be able to light the candle. Roll the wax over the wick, pressing lightly along the entire piece of wick. Continue to roll the remainder of the wax. When rolling is completed, smooth the edge of the wax by gently pressing the seam down, being careful not to crush the candle.

Nishmat

BY RABBI ARTHUR WASKOW

You Whose very Name—
YyyyHhhhWwwwHhhh—
Is the Breath of Life,
The breathing of all life
Gives joy and blessing to Your Name.

As lovers lie within each other's arms,
Whispering each the other's name
Into the other's ear, So we lie in Your arms,
Breathing with each breath
Your Name, Your Truth, Your Unity.

You alone,
Your Breath of Life alone,
Guides us,
Frees us,
Transforms us, Heals us,
Nurtures us,
Teaches us.

First, last,
Future, past,
Inward, outward,
Beyond, between,
You are the breathing that gives life to all the worlds.
And we do the breathing that gives life to all the worlds.

As we breathe out what the trees breathe in,
And the trees breathe out what we breathe in,
So we breathe each other into life,
We and You.

YyyyHhhhWwwwHhhh.

Havdallah

At the conclusion of Shabbat we mark the entry back into the work week with the brief ceremony of *Havdallah*, which means "separation."

Bring out a special wine, (or juice for the children,) light candles and scent your home with sweet smells, perhaps some oils burning in an oil-burner or some incense. Create a beautiful atmosphere to end the Sabbath. The home is still in festive mood and we take the sweetness of Sabbath into the rest of our week to help sustain us even as we are savoring the last moments of our day of rest.

Havdallah is about closure and transition; from one beautiful moment to the next, even though both moments may be entirely different from each other. When we look for guidance to create a ritual in our life to honor closure and separation, we can draw inspiration from *Havdallah* and understand that a simple ceremony can help us make the necessary transition.

Try ending your Sabbaths with *Havdallah* and bring the strength of the holy day to your children's lives at school and your own lives at work. It is a special blessing of separation and it will remain in your heart throughout the week like a guardian to protect your moments that form your busy week.

In our home we can put the *Havdallah* candle on a dish of warmed brandy. This way it ignites and we can sing "Shavuah tov" (a good week) to the departing Shabbat until the flame flickers and dies.

The Dream

A READING-ALOUD STORY FOR HAVDALLAH

BY NAOMI STEINBERG

Once there was a woman who had been walking through the desert for forty years, when at last she arrived at the boundary of the Land of Understanding. But before entering that country, it was necessary first to cross an endless lake of tears. The woman stepped into the water and swam.

She swam for forty years, and when she emerged on the opposite shore she was a very old woman. She dropped to her knees and kissed the holy ground. And as she opened her eyes she saw in front of her the feet of the Prophet Elijah. And the Prophet Elijah lifted her up and held out a golden goblet full of wine. Then the Prophet Elijah raised the goblet and pronounced the blessing to God. And they passed the cup of joy back and forth, the two of them drinking deeply, until the woman became completely intoxicated and sank to the ground and fell asleep.

And as she slept she dreamt that she was again crossing the desert. But this time the Prophet Elijah walked in front of her, and forty years passed like an instant. When they arrived at the boundary of the Land of Understanding, the prophet Elijah spread out his mantle, and the lake of tears parted, and they walked effortlessly across.

Arriving on the opposite shore, they dropped to their knees and kissed the holy ground. And when they opened their eyes they saw in front of them the feet of the Shechinah herself. And the Shechinah lifted them up, and held out a crystal goblet full of

Judith Hankin.

wine. And the Shechinah raised the goblet and pronounced the blessing to God.

And they passed the cup of joy around, the three of them drinking deeply, until the prophet Elijah and the woman became completely intoxicated and sank to the ground. And there, with the Shechinah watching over them, they fell into a deep, dreamless sleep, from which they have yet to be awakened.

Blessed is the Creative, *flowing lovingly into time and space, numbers and patterns, that has evolved us to the level of complexity admitting awareness of beauty, wonder, and awe.*

Blessings for Special Occasions

Judaism has often been called the Blessing Way, a powerful image for a spiritual path that links each one of us to the greater whole and to God the ancient Holy One through blessing. Blessing in the Judaic tradition is a way of life, and a personal empowering energy that can be awakened within our deepest self to infuse all life with joy, strength, and inspiration. In this section you will read articles on blessing by different contributors. You will find brief biographical details on the authors at the back of the book in the section entitled List of Contributors, together with their addresses and contact numbers.

THE POWER OF BLESSING

BY JONATHAN OMER-MAN AND SHOHAMA WIENER

Blessings are the manifestation of life's continuous renewal. The whole universe is held together by a multidimensional, ever-expanding circle of blessing, all of which emanates from the Divine Nature of creation. The circle of blessing nourishes our lives with sustenance, joy, and enrichment in a myriad of forms, from the food we eat, to the seasons of our lives, to the seeds of our generations, to the experience of community, to the creativity of our arts and sciences, to the *mitzvot* that we perform, and on and on.

As the individual and collective human beings that we are, a major part of our mission in this world is to create, energize, and amplify the circle of blessing. Our blessings have power. Our special attribute is that we are programmed with the stuff of the Holy One, blessed be the name, and thus are enabled to consciously expand the common pool of blessing in the world. Our ability to glue blessing and to plug into the Divine Unfolding with our blessings and prayers is perhaps the single greatest attribute that defines our creation in the image of God.

The totality of Jewish life is structured so that we are continually resonating with the blessing in our lives and expanding and regenerating the pool of blessing in the universe. As a people, our active relationship to the act of blessing has enabled us to survive and flourish during the most difficult and oppressive of times. On a deeper level, the continuing and ongoing contribution to the pool of blessing by all peoples strengthens the cosmic building blocks that hold the universe together.

Our blessings have power. When we partake of food or celebrate our days or express our gratitude, we nourish the Divine Blesser when either silently or aloud we voice our appreciation through blessing for specific gifts of the Great Good that fills our lives and all the worlds at that specific moment.

Our blessings have power. Our blessings pierce other worlds as we extend the divine spark within us to the souls of our loved ones who have departed this dimension.

Our blessings have power. By harmonizing our will to the possibilities latent in the natural order of things, we bless the earth and the universe to bring forth its bounty, to bring peace and healing and to give protection to our lives and those for whom we care.

Our blessings have power. By focusing our consciousness, opening our hearts, envisioning latent possibilities, invoking holy images, and directing our intentions, we are able to envision healing and regeneration and seek these in ourselves, in others, and in the Cosmic Being.

Our blessings have power because they connect us to the power source of the universe. As Adam, the one being embodying both genders that is created in the likeness of the Divine, we are capable of catalyzing transformation and regeneration through the simple act of giving our blessing.

The Scroll of Esther, *Galicia, twentieth century. Jewish Museum, New York.*

SOME GUIDING CONCEPTS FOR
DEREKH HABRACHOT—THE BLESSING PATH
BY JONATHAN OMER-MAN AND SHOHAMA WEINER

The *Etz Chaim,* the Tree of Life, is the power symbol of the blessing way. It bas been with us throughout the totality of human experience to keep us connected to the source of all blessing and to teach us how to live so that we are always connected. We must always remember that our connection to the *Etz Chaim* is as near as our heart.

The more we give blessings, the greater our skill becomes. Constantly practice giving blessings. Speak blessings of praise, thanksgiving, and wonder. Offer blessings of well wishing, hope, and comfort.

We need to always act as if we believe in the power of blessing to heal and to transform. Even when our objective reality says a situation is devoid of hope, seek out the tiniest light of possibility, and concentrate on that as the focal point of our blessing.

In voicing our blessings, we must always be sensitive to the recipient. As we used to say in the sixties, "Don't lay a trip on anyone." We need to frame our blessings in terms that can be heard and welcomed. If the recipient is closed to hearing a blessing from us, speak it silently. If our blessing is said in a way that provokes resistance in the one for whom it is intended, the resistance will diminish its power.

When we give a blessing, we are more than ourselves. We bring the intention. The blessing itself comes from the Source of All Blessing. In the process of formulating a blessing we need to make ourselves quiet, even for an instant, so we can allow the blessing to formulate itself.

In the act of blessing, we give name and form to something that is either latent or already exists to facilitate its manifestation in this world.

We must encourage ourselves not to be angry at, or to judge others for the places where they are broken. When we commit ourselves to *Derekh Habrachot,* our perceptions of negativity become our reference point for the formulation of blessing. It is our task to strive to transform what we see through the act of blessing. The act of judgment belongs to the one true judge, blessed be His name.

Shonna Husbands-Hankin.

THE SIMCHA CUP

BY SHONNA HUSBANDS-HANKIN

There are many layers to the telling of a story, to the sharing of
a blessing. Each layer of telling is a gateway to the next level of
understanding. And each level of experience adds to the cumula-
tive insights, revealing wonder. Such is the story of the Simcha
Cup.

This could really be the story of our dear Rebbe Shlomo
Carlebeach and how he brought together special energy and drew
out amazing gifts of precious stones from a stranger to us as a
wedding couple at our wedding meal. Or it could be a story of
how an event of a baby naming turned into another wedding
instead, at which Reb Zalman Schacter-Shalomi officiated. Or
it could be the story of how thousands of people are connected
to each other through the presence, the radiance of a special cup.
It is all of these and more. But for now, a simple version.

A handmade silver goblet adorned with precious stones of
opals, garnets, and other jewels has become a cup of blessing for
thousands of people. Its opal stones were initially offered as a
wedding gift to my husband and me in 1977 by an Israeli man,
Gidon, along with the blessing that "our children should never
know want." These precious stones we gave a few years later as a
wedding gift to our friends Shira and Hananya Kronenberg, with
the blessing to create something to share with community. In the
hands of Shira the artist, a magnificent cup was fashioned.

That spring, in 1980, our first daughter, Talya, was born, and
we worked to create a meaningful naming ceremony for her, to be
held in the forest close to our home. Shira was planning to bring
the cup and surprise us at the ceremony. By a great miracle, at the
exact day and time and same location, the wedding of our dear
friends Judith Hankin and Jesse Rappaport was to be held. So it
was that under their chuppah, with the guidance of Rabbis
Zalman Schacter-Shalomi and Daniel Siegel, that the Simcha Cup
was first initiated into the community circle of blessing.

And so, the Simcha Cup was sanctified as the *kiddush gadol* cup for an extended network of family and friends in the Pacific Northwest. Over its twenty-year journey, it has traveled to a few hundred *simchas*—baby namings, Brises, Bar and Bat mitzvahs, weddings, anniversaries, Rosh Chodesh rituals, young women's first-moon ceremonies, rabbinic ordinations, Eshet Hazon ceremonies, and more. It has been hand-carried across North America, being zapped by the photo detection devices at airports numerous times. It has journeyed to Israel as well for Talya's Bat Mitzvah in Jerusalem. The special protection and delivery of the cup has created networks among strangers and a web of sacred connections between people, places, and sacred events.

The cup has a life of its own. It has an invisible tether and a place of belonging in our Shabbat cupboard. But we do not "own it." Requests come for its presence to grace the next *simcha* event, near and far. It always must be hand-carried and escorted with tender loving care. It travels in a small wooden box, a gift from one of the wedding couples who used it, and is wrapped in a long woven band of colored fabric. Among other things, it had a several-year sojourn in Vancouver, B.C., with the *havurah* there in its earlier lifetime. And once it was hand-carried from a Bar Mitzvah in Vancouver, B.C., to a rendezvous point in Washington D.C., where it was driven

Kiddush cup *from Jerusalem, 1964.*
Ludwig Wolpert. Jewish Museum,
New York.

to a rabbinic ordination the next day in Philadelphia. Along its
amazing journey we kept a list in the box of who had used it and
where it had traveled; the list was lost, a new one started, then
lost again. Apparently the cup is not meant to have a solid record,
but rather to be a mystical, magical story. Know that there are
thousands of people out there who have seen and used this cup at
special events, who have sipped kiddush from the joy that it has
brought. Maybe one day, too, you will be blessed with the cup, as
it blesses you back with its presence. Or maybe you will create
your own cup for your own community to share.

But keep your eye out for this Simcha Cup. For its travels
are wide and it has blessed a lot of people. This year the cup will
come full circle, for its presence has been requested at two Bar
Mitzvahs, one in Boise, Idaho, the other in either Colorado or
Jerusalem. The two *simchas*? That of the son of the cupmaker,
Zev Nachman Kroneneberg, and that of the son of one of the
rabbis who officiated at its first use, Yotam Schachter-Shalomi.
But maybe the names don't matter. Nor the places. For the two
boys don't know each other but are woven together, just like the
thousands of others who are connected by the mystery of the
Simcha Cup.

May it always be a Blessing as it passes Blessing among us.
And when we are long gone and the cup still remains, may there
always be someone to tell the story. And may our children never
know want.

Avrum Davis.

An Artist's Blessing

PREPARING THE WAY

BY SHONNA HUSBANDS-HANKIN

A Blessing Ritual for those using their Hands in healing touch and sacred creative expression. Hamsa hand. Healing hand. Creative hand. Artist of the hand and heart. A blessing for the energy that flows through us. As we prepare to open ourselves to the light of radiant energy that flows from above, we prepare our heats to receive, our minds to formulate, our senses to be open, our hands to express. We are but temporary vessels for the creative energy of the universe to crystallize and manifest through the touch and expression of our hands.

167

Ketubah, *a Jewish marriage contract made for a bride and groom in Constantinople, in 1853. Israel Museum, Jerusalem.*

Hands. Those extensions of our being that connect us to this world. Hands. Those amazingly mundane yet special beings that can sense and touch, hold and heal, write and draw, paint and sculpt, move and express, cook and clean, carry and crush, hold and hurt. And so much more. As we ready ourselves to do holy work with our hands, whether in the form of artistic expression or a sacred healing work, we must ready our whole beings. In creating a sacred space to do Judaic artwork, as I usher my classes into the territory of painting their own silk *tallitot, hallah* covers, or creating any sacred pieces, I have come to feel the need to stop for a moment first, to meditate and reflect on what we are embarking

to do. To realize and remember that it is not just "you" who are
the power manifesting your creative expression. That God is play-
ing a role in the larger "creation" of which we are each a part.

So, the brief ritual I share is that of a sacred hand-washing to
prepare oneself to "pray with the hands of creation and healing."
In a class or group setting, we gather in a circle and gently sing
or hum the song "Wings of peace" (by R. Aryeh Hirschfield),
while I ritually wash each person's hands with the special Shabbat
hand-washing cup. Then, raising our hands up above our heads,
together we recite the traditional blessing for hand-washing (in
any gender format you wish):

Baruch Ata Yah, E'oheynu Ruach Ha Olam
Asher K'DShanu B'Mitzvotav, Vitzevanu
Al Netilat Yadayim
Blessed are you Ru-Eng Spirit of the world who commands us to lift up our hands

I then offer each person their precious white silk, or other art
materials, and we move into the creation phase in silence, in
order to allow for transition and to carry forth the sense of spirituality in our work

As a closing at the end of class together, in pairs, we offer a
personal blessing of the hand and heart. Placing our left hands
on our hearts and joining the palms of our right hands to those
of our partners, we offer a personal blessing of creativity, insight,
and healing to each other. In that way, the strand of spiritual
energy is given honor and connects us through our collective
creative journey.

May S/he who dwells on high and among us continue to
let flow the expressive qualities of light and love, as our hands
bring forth the fruits of our spirit of imagination, creativity,
and healing.

I Went Down to the Nut Garden
by Judith Hankin.

UNTITLED

> *A poem is an awakening*
> *a glimpse into the soul*
> *an expression of the beyond,*
> *a tale of that which cannot be told.*
>
> *It is an image,*
> *a scribble of the pen,*
> *a weaving of the worlds,*
> *the flowers of spring and fall*
> *blooming in the snow.*
> > –MONIQUE PASTERNAK

BERAKHOT BEFORE FOOD

Barukh attah adonai eloheinu melekh ha-olam, ha-motzi lehem min ha-atz
Blessed are You, Source of the Universe who brings forth bread from the earth.

Barakh attah adonai eloheinu melekh ha-olam, bo-re minei m'zonot.
Blessed are You, Source of the Universe who creates various kinds of nourishment.

Barukh attah adonai eloheinu melekh ha-olam, bo-re p'ri ha-gafen.
Blessed are You, Source of the Universe who creates fruit of the vine.

Barukh attah adonai eloheinu melekh ha-olam, bo-re p'ri ha-etz.
Blessed are You, Source of the Universe who creates fruit of the tree.

Barukh attah adonai eloheinu melekh ha-olam, bo-re p'ri ha-adamah.
Blessed are You, Source of the Universe who creates fruit of the ground.

Barukh attah adonai eloheinu melekh ha-olam, she-ha-kol nihyeh bi-d'varo
Blessed are You, Source of the Universe at whose word all things come into being.

BLESSING FOR TRAVELERS

May it be Your will, Source of the Universe,
to lead us on the way of peace and guide and direct
so that You will bring us happily
to our destination, safe and sound.
Save us from danger on the way.
Give us good grace, kindness and favor
in both Your eyes and the eyes of all those we meet.
Hear this our prayer, for You are a God who
listens to the heart's requests and communion.
Blessed are You, Source of the Universe.

BLESSINGS FOR VARIOUS OCCASIONS

Barukh attah adonai eloheinu melekh ha-o'am, bo-re minei v'samim.
Blessed are You, Source of the Universe who creates various spices.

Barukh attah adonai eloheinu melekh ha-o'am, bo-re atzei v'samim.
Blessed are You, Source of the Universe who creates fragrant trees.

Barukh attah adonai eloheinu melekh ha-o'am, bo-re isvei v'samim.
Blessed are You, Source of the Universe who creates fragrant plants.

Barukh attah adonai eloheinu melekh ha-o'am, ha-noten rei-ah tov ba-perot.
Blessed are You, Source of the Universe who gives a pleasant fragrance to fruits.

Barukh attah adonai eloheinu melekh ha-o'am, bo-re shemen arev.
Blessed are You, Source of the Universe who creates fragrant oil.

Judith Hankin.

PRAYER FOR HEALING THROUGH MEDICINE
BY YITZHAK HUSBANDS-HANKIN

I use this blessing from the weekday Amidah, for taking medicine.
It is in appreciation of God's healing that comes through medi-
cines, and to make taking medicine a holy act, by thanking the
Creator as the source of healing. I use this payer in order to more
deeply invite the wholeness of the gift of healing into my being,
along with the medicine.

Baruch Atah Adonai, Eloheynu Melech Ha Olam
Rofeh Choley Amo Yisrael.

Blessed are You, Holy One, Life of the Universe
Who Heals Among the People Israel.

BLESSING FOR INVOKING CELESTIAL GUIDES
BY RABBI LEAH NOVICK

This blessing is suitable both for individuals seeking to become
connected with their personal guidance and for those who regu-
larly invoke guides or the presence of angels.

Women say—Hin'ni muchana u'm'zumana
or men say—Hin'ni muchan u'm'zuman
L'kabeyl et ha madrichim ha elyonim v'ha kedoshim sheli
b'ahava u'b kavod. Bruchim habaim, bruchot ha baot.

I hereby declare myself prepared and ready
to receive my transcendent and holy guides,
with great love and respect.
Welcome, divine visitors.

BEDTIME PRAYERS
BY NAOMI STEINBERG

My son and I softly say the following Hebrew lines to each other as a back-and-forth blessing when I tuck him in bed. A sweet way to end the day. From the traditional bedtime prayers:

Baruch Adonai b'yom
Baruch Adonai b'lailah
Baruch Adonaib'shachvaynu
Baruch Adonai b'kumaynu

Blessed is the Holy One by day,
Blessed is the Holy One by night,
Blessed is the Holy One when we lie down,
Blessed is the Holy One when we rise up.

BEDTIME BLESSING

May I (you) be guarded on every side by the angels of God and above me (you) and all around me (you) the Shechinah.

The Kaballah.

New Rituals and Celebrations

In this section you will find a few pieces by different authors on how to create new rituals of celebration. Many are teachers, rabbis, or simply individuals who have found meaning and depth in ritual making and have adapted ancient traditions to modern times to hearten and bond their communities. We hope that their stories and words will be an encouragement and an inspiration for you also, to make your days holy, joyful, and full. You will find brief biographical details on the contributors at the end of the book in the section entitled "List of Contributors," together with a list of addresses and contacts.

CREATING OUR OWN BLESSING
BY MARCIA COHN SPIEGEL

Reciting a blessing allows us to open ourselves to God's presence in our lives. The act of blessing is one of turning to that which is beyond our ability to understand and recognizing our own limitations. Many of us are not aware of the number and variety of blessings that have been created over the ages to acknowledge special moments in our lives: seeing a rainbow, eating the first fruit of the season, learning of the death of a loved one, surviving

The Scroll of Esther (*detail*) *by Shalom d'Halia.*
Jewish Museum, New York.

an earthquake or thunderstorm, as well as the mundane act of
eating each daily meal. The rabbis even created a blessing for
drinking water.

Sometimes we are moved to say a spontaneous blessing but
don't know the traditional prayer for this occasion or event. I
have found that people who are struggling, ill, or facing a crisis,
may want to pray but may not know the language of prayer, nor
do they see a blessing in their pain. At these times it is helpful to
have a model for creating our own blessing or prayer, based on

the ancient formula, but mirroring our own language, philosophy, and perception of God's place in our lives. The process that I use is simple, and I have found it to be particularly effective for people who are not observant or have been out of touch with regular religious practice in their lives. We start by remembering the traditional blessing formula *(Blessed art thou, Lord of the Universe, who has...)* and think about what names we choose for God. We define for ourselves what God's power, qualities, and attributes are. We state the act, event, or circumstances for which we want a blessing, and finally we reiterate God's ability to act in the world.

The following blessing, conceived by a woman who prayed to heal a misunderstanding with an alienated adult child, adheres to the proposed model:

1. (Naming God) Blessed are You, Shekina,
2. (Quality and attribute) who nurtures and protects us all;
3. (Event) be with me as I reach out to embrace my child.
4. (God's ability to act) Blessed are you who binds up our wounds.

The act of creating this blessing helped the woman realize that she could not pray for healing from a male god. She wanted a soothing presence that surrounded her, protected her, and empowered to act, and she found this in the image of Shekina. The comfort of this image and the blessing eased her anxiety and gave her spiritual encouragement and support. She went to the meeting wrapped in the wings of the Shekina.

We may need to be reminded that blessing and prayer are the starting point for our own dialogue with the Creator and give ourselves permission to be personal in our prayers.

OLD SYMBOLS, NEW RITUALS
ADAPTING TRADITIONAL SYMBOLS, CEREMONIES, AND BLESSINGS

We have invented new ceremonies, created new music and songs,
new ways to celebrate with a sense of the tradition from which
they are drawn. We have adapted traditional rituals and expanded
the meaning of traditional blessings. We have dared to write
new prayers.

1. CREATE A SACRED SPACE

In the wilderness the Jewish people built a *mishkan*, a portable
sanctuary. All participated in its creation by weaving cloth,
making ritual vessels, beautifying the holy place. Before we begin
our ceremony we must crate our own *mishkan*. Consider how you
make the space holy for the time you will be using it. Form a
circle, delineating the boundaries with ribbons or flowers, drape
fabric or *tallit* around to define the area, hold or braid ribbons
together. Flowers, fabrics, music, scents, are all tools to create
your *mishkan*.

2. CREATE A MOOD

To transition from the outside world to this special moment,
silence or subdued background music are helpful. Begin with a
song. It is wise to explain at the outset what is about to take place.
Your ceremony will have at least three parts: the opening, the
body of the ritual, and the closing. Consider the amount of time
your ceremony will take; half an hour or less for a simple ritual
to as long as an hour and a half is comfortable.

3. Select Components for the Ritual

The following list includes many familiar aspects drawn from ceremonies and services

- Candle lighting
- Kiddush, blessing wine or grape juice
- Hallah, blessing bread
- Spices
- Hand-washing
- Foot-washing (as Abraham did with the angels)
- Planting a tree for future generations, particularly appropriate for births, birthdays, weddings, healing
- Blessing special foods: first fruit of season, ceremonial foods
- Giving a gift of charity
- Making a vow of service or good deeds to the community
- Changing a name as Avram and Sarai did when they became Abraham and Sarah
- Wearing a special garment such as a *tallit* or changing a garment
- Cutting. Tradition says that we "cut a covenant" (the *brit* or circumcision)
- Reading, studying, and interpreting a text from Torah
- Chanting from the Torah in English or Hebrew
- Storytelling, or the act of each person adding a piece to the story
- Exchanging, giving gifts
- Creating amulets
- Singing, learning new songs
- Dancing
- Prayers and blessings, both familiar and newly created
- *Mikveh*, immersion in water—hot tub, pool, etc.
- Anointing, use of water or oil—i.e., put some on eyelids, say, "I bless your eyes that you may see visions of peace, etc."
- Guided meditation or guided visualization
- Silence. It can be very powerful.

4. Addressing Anger, Pain, and Sorrow

Each Jewish holiday has its own special symbols which can be used or adapted.

- Emptying our pockets and casting the debris into the water, symbolizing cleansing ourselves
- At a funeral mourners rip their garments in grief. The tearing of cloth is very powerful
- Before a wedding a plate is broken, during the wedding the groom steps on a glass to break it
- Keening, shouting, moaning may be an expression of anger or sorrow
- At the close of the Sabbath, Havdalah is performed to separate the holy from the routine. The use of spices, candles, and wine is a fine way to separate one event from another
- These acts of burning, tearing, cleaning, casting out, breaking, stamping, cleansing, moving can allow us to do symbolically what we would like to do in our own lives.

5. Ceremonial Objects

The use of ritual objects, garments, or other treasures from family members or friends which have historic or nostalgic connections, can add a moving note to any ritual.

6. Questions to Contemplate

For many rituals it is appropriate to think of answering three.

- What do you want to leave behind?
- What do you want to remember or take with you from the past?
- What do you want to create new for the future?

You may create new questions, or reframe these.

Creating a Women's Rosh Chodesh Ceremony

BY YEHUDIT STEINBERG-CAUDILL

The Rosh Chodesh Ceremony is a wonderful opportunity for women and girls to gather monthly. During this time, we can be very innovative in the creation of our rituals. This is a renewal process of an ancient oral tradition. Since most of the forgotten women's rituals were handed down from generation to generation orally, it is up to us in this time-period to set the stage as to how Rosh Chodesh will be celebrated in future generations.

Rosh Chodesh is the ushering of the New Month, *Rosh* meaning "head" in Hebrew and *Chodesh* meaning "month." This is an ancient Jewish women's holy day to embrace our feminine spirit, coinciding with the new moon. The essence of this monthly ceremony is to honor the rebirthing process in our lives. We are experimenting with ways to create Jewish women's rituals in an egalitarian, creative, expressive-arts mode. Rosh Chodesh was given as a half holiday for women as it is said they did not give their gold for the making of the golden calf.

The goal for each month is to create a Jewish Women's psycho-spiritual transformation ceremony that incorporates the unique quality of each Hebrew month. Done on a yearly cyclical basis, we begin to live within the ancient Hebrew cycle. An awareness and deeper understanding of our whole person begins to emerge. When studying the upcoming Hebrew month at our planning meetings, we search for the thread of transformational process that lies within the teachings of the each month. The psycho-spiritual transformational process underlying Jewish theology becomes apparent to us as we begin to live and celebrate this system.

Clues for creating ceremonial rituals are found by identifying monthly holidays and associated biblical stories about women. We can locate stories within the Torah readings for the month and study the holiday stories. Once the intentionality of the month has been identified, we can then pursue the psycho-spiritual

Judith Hankin.

essence of this time in the Jewish cyclical calendar. Discussion concerns how we can incorporate the symbols into a thematic ritual, and we look for ways to deepen our personal and communal awareness.

There are many different ways to organize a Rosh Chodesh Group. Some groups take this opportunity to study text together, while others create a *mishpacha* (family), which meets monthly. Our group has chosen to create community through developing a monthly ceremony on the Erev (eve) of Rosh Chodesh. Because Jewish days begin at sundown, the "new beginning" is in the evening, when darkness first appears. This correlates with the natural cycle of the new moon. Called "darkness before the dawn," the new moon is a time to honor the shadows.

The ceremony is held on the night when one can first see the sliver of the moon, during its cycle of growing toward fullness. An important ritual for this group is to perform a ceremony at the time of the intentionality of the holiday (on the actual night). Since our Jewish Calendar is based on a lunar as well as solar calendar, each month the evening celebration changes. Some groups choose to have a set monthly meeting near the Rosh Chodesh holiday in order to accommodate their members' busy schedules. Our group is attempting to live within the energy of the natural cycles; therefore we hold our monthly ceremonies on the actual holiday. Another characteristic of our group is a total open-door policy. All women and girls are welcome to attend the celebration. We are a group of women who gather on the eve of the Jewish new month to celebrate and honor ourselves, our community and our heritage. We are an open, egalitarian, nondenominational, multigenerational, all-inclusive, unaffiliated group of San Francisco Bay Area Jewish Women. We encourage participation, at whatever level the women are comfortable. Some help in the planning, room setup, phone calling, and so forth, while others show up for the event and are very welcome to "just be" without obligations. We have several dedicated planners who are willing to give time to the preparation.

Seven-branched candelabrum *from Hungary, 1922. Jewish Museum, New York.*

After three years of continuous involvement within the
Rosh Chodesh cycles, a deeper richness has occurred in my life.
Through a series of intuitive insights, an engaging process
emerged from deep within
my being. This flash of
Shekina energy opened
the gates of my under-
standing of the indwelling
presence. This ancient Inner
Presence of the divine feminine
attribute of the one God we call
Shekina becomes the living dance
in this physical reality.
At this moment of connection,
along with the acknowledgment and
awareness of my physical environment,
a surge of joyful feelings rose up from the
base of my feet and spread throughout my
entire body, and I felt truly alive. Singing, dancing, and honoring all that is. And in that moment,
I saw the ancestral mothers up on the mountain. I heard their
voices calling. They brought wisdom teachings from the past. As
we begin to open to them, we bring their presence into our ceremonies. When this connection occurs, it provides the opportunity for each member of the group to take a moment
and listen to those who have come before us.
Dance and movement can be an important
part of this ceremony. The rhythms of our
ancestors from the Middle East, Persia
and Northern Africa speak to our feminine
spirits. The essential experience of dancing
and feeling these rhythms helps us to remember our forgotten mysteries. Middle Eastern
dance is the dance of our Ancestors. Because we

wandered in the wilderness desert for forty years, we come from Semitic tribal lifestyles. Twelve tribes around the Holy Mishkan (Sacred Center) that housed the Ark of the covenant: these are the indigenous roots of our people. We are proud of the aliveness of the Shekina. She dances and sings, lover of life, like the heat dances off the desert earth. The Rosh Chodesh Ceremony is the ritual of ancestral mothers. When we play the music, sing the native language, and dance the native dance, we become alive. Too many years has our spirit been imprisoned. Now is the time to awaken to the Divine Energy within each and everyone of us, the eternal mystery that manifests itself in the exotic melodies and rhythms of our Bedouin ancestors. Our tradition is so rich in expressive creative art. Our Jewish tradition traverses the globe, with multicultural dimensions yet to be explored. Acknowledging and exploring the Semitic influences within our indigenous roots, which come from the Sinai Desert, provides a depth of understanding that transcends time. Our archetypal selves call out to us from deep within. The journey of the soul begins to recapture our roots from the primordial Tree of Life. This is the concept we experiment with when creating and conducting our ceremonies.

One question to ask ourselves is, What was it like to live a Bedouin lifestyle? A nomadic tribe moves continually, setting up camp, breaking camp, and forging on into the wilderness, not really knowing what tomorrow has in store. They live simply and yet have many survival and safety concerns daily. When we engage in active-imagination experiences, transformation does occur. Having a group ritual creates bonds, and community begins to grow within the group. It is time to restore the balance of the garden. Stop and smell the roses, stop a moment and take a look at the sky, the clouds, and take a deep breath, thanking the Mother Earth and the Shekina, the recognition of the Divine Presence in our lives.

It is time for women to get back in touch with their feminine soul and balance their energies—the energies of giving and receiving. Exploring sensuality, opening our hearts to the beauties of life, we can create a life filled with meaning, artistic moments of wonderment, and a heartfelt zest for life. At the base of Jewish theology lies the spiritual presence in this world. Judaism is practiced in the here and now. Its entire premise is that we can have an active part in the changing of this world to make a better place for all humanity. Shekina is an allowing, receiving, open, spontaneous, doing energy. She floats with synchronicity through our day and gives birth to ideas and thoughts. Creating Sacred Space in a Jewish context requires preparation to enter into creative space. Through the formation of sacred space, moving into altered states of consciousness and then into the creation of a ritual, we allow ourselves to engage in the creation process The "allowing" is the clue for creative preparation.

The first requirement for creative being is receptivity. Creative ideas do not seem to come by searching for them however; if we are not open to receive them, they will not come. Creative ideas are not necessarily under our voluntary control, yet they require that we be in a certain space to receive them. The original ideas come to us "like foreign guests," as Goethe said. Receptivity involves detaching oneself from one's ongoing concerns and, without particular expectations, heeding the ideas that come. Expressive dance, chanting, and silent meditation are some of the modes that assist this process. Receptivity to ideas also demands that they be actively welcomed. Another condition for the creative process to occur is to immerse oneself in a single focus. Mantra meditations and repetitive chants or words help to focus attention inward. Creative work seems to demand both passionate interest and a certain degree of detachment.

The leadership model we experiment with is one of group leadership. The group has been working on a ceremony format that can be replicated monthly. While providing the presenters with a basic formula for creating a Rosh Chodesh ceremony, this format allows for innovation and the creation of a unique ritual. The ceremony is divided into four parts—Opening the Circle, Creating Sacred Space, Monthly Ritual, and Closing—and lasts two hours.

PART 1: OPENING THE CIRCLE

We begin with a chant followed by three to five minutes of silent meditation. This serves to bring focus to the group as well as proclaim that something different is going to occur. Next we announce the New Month: Rosh Chodesh, the ushering in of the New Month, an ancient Jewish women's holy day to embrace our feminine spirit, coinciding with the new moon. We now begin the opening of our ceremony for this new month of —— .

We begin by the lighting of candles, using any number of creative means to enhance the process. Sometimes I use a seven-branch menorah in the center of the circle; other times we have a sand-filled aluminum tray of votive candles for every member to light; sometimes we float candles in water, a lunar symbol. We recite a feminine blessing;

Judith Hankin.

Brucha at Yah, Eloheynu
Tevarcheynu ve'tishme'reynu
tachat knafey ha'Shekina,
vetadlik eysh benafsheynua al yedey
hadlakat hanerot heldu shel Rosh Chodesh

Blessed are you, our God,
Who blesses us and protects us under the wings of the Shekhina,
and lights a flame in our souls,
as through the lighting of these Rosh Chodesh candles.

A poem read by one of the group members is appropriate at this time. This concludes opening the circle. We allow approximately fifteen minutes for this section.

PART 2: CREATING SACRED SPACE

HONORING THE DIRECTIONS

As in many indigenous, agrarian ceremonial traditions, we honor the directions. In a Jewish context we begin with the east, move to the south, west, north, above and below. We have tried to be innovative in performing this ritual, applying the symbolism of the Mishkan (portable sanctuary in the wilderness that housed the Ark of the

189

Covenant) in several different ways. Animal symbols exist for the directions, and certain astrological signs correlate with the twelve ancestral tribes, as do certain feminine ancestors.

On Sukkot we use the *lulav* to salute the six directions.

PURIFICATION THROUGH HAND-WASHING

Hand-washing is a substitute for the monthly *mikveh* (Jewish water-immersion ritual). We pass a hand-washing cup and bowl, to which rose water or another scent has been added. We sing and chant as we ritually wash our hands. *Shefta Mayim* is a good song here. We also repeat the traditional blessing for hand-washing:

Brucha at Yah, Shekinah al natilat ya dayim.

May the source of blessings, Shekina, purify us—
this symbolized by the washing of our hands.

PERSONAL INTRODUCTIONS

In this part of the ceremony each person in the circle has a chance to say her name and briefly introduce herself. She is asked to invite the spirits of her mothers and female relatives, teachers, and friends to the circle for the ceremony.

MONTHLY BLESSING AND INTENTION

We create a blessing and intention for this particular month, which sets the stage for the ritual that is about to occur.

TRANSITION CHANT, OR NIGGUN

PART 3: THE RITUAL

The central ritual part of the ceremony is different every month.
A variety of activities that include the creative imagination occur
during this time. We allow about an hour, maybe a little longer
depending on the month and what the activity is for that month.
We employ creative visual-arts projects, Hebrew letters, movement, storytelling, psycho-spiritual process writing. Included in
this section is a meditation, chanting, dancing, or movement of
some sort.

PART 4: CLOSING THE CIRCLE

We close the circle by saying good-bye to our ancestor guests.
We read collectively... It is the women who have kept the Torah
pure, who have brought teachings down through the ages, from
generation to generation. *L'dor v'dor*. It is the women who said "no"
to participating in the building of the golden calf. And if it had
not been for our maternal ancestors, we would not be teaching
Torah today, and it is up to us to continue to teach the wisdom to
our children and encourage them to teach it to their children.
So it is and so may it be. Amen.

   We sing a closing song such as *Hene Ma Tov Uma Nain*.

Finally, we end every monthly Rosh Chodesh ceremony with a
dessert potluck and socializing.

PART III

The Life Cycle

TURNED MY MOURNING INTO DANCING

by YEHUDIT STEINBERG-CAUDILL

A long time ago, the Jewish people were dancin' folks. We danced at even the bittersweet moments. Dancing and singing in circles amongst ourselves, the men together in circles and the women together in circles and spirals. Moving and swaying, clapping and singing, together in community. Body, mind, and spirit engaged in the celebration of life-cycle events.

Today, as the "resurgence of spirit" creeps back into our community, once again we begin to dance. Uncrossing our arms and legs, untangling the hurt from within, letting go of our encrusted inhibitions, we once again begin to sing and dance. And as we move into the rhythm of the *niggun* (a wordless Hasidic melody), something deep inside makes connection with the ancestors. The tears begin to flow from a place deep down inside and I know not why. I allow the bittersweet sorrow to rise from the depths of my soul as we continue to dance. The Hasidic *niggun* melody takes over my entire being.

I begin to feel lighter. A sense of joy encompasses my entire being, releasing pent-up emotions that have been lying dormant within for many years. Touching the archetypal Jewish soul lets me know I have returned home. Suddenly, a wave of compassion overcomes my entire being. The feelings of anger transform, almost instantaneously, to sadness. This sadness is not for myself, but for the entire community.

I feel the oppression of our ancestors as if I was living it right now. And I cry, deep, deep sobs. In another instant, a big sigh of relief flows through and surrounds my body. Singing and dancing become even more meaningful and I "lose myself." Freedom from my thoughts and the everyday worries leave. A surge of joy flows through my entire being as I celebrate this dance. I am still dancing the ancestors' dance and singing the community's song. I have turned my mourning into dancing. All that is left is the *niggun* and the dance.

Naming

The choice of a child's name begins to shape their future. It is one of the first choices we make for a child, and is a very important one. By placing this important choice within a Jewish context, you have already begun to give your child an identity, a community, and a way of being in the world. A name is a gift with many dimensions. Almost all Jewish names are links to some biblical aspect, placing the child in the context of an ancient but still living story. Indeed, because of the tribal nature of Judaism, these biblical names are names of blood relatives and ancestors.

In the Bible, naming is the very first independent human act—Adam names the animals, birds, and every living thing. For humans there is something entirely mystical about naming, and in fact many of the great sages of our history were particularly good at giving names that became appropriate to the growing child, as though the future was laid out by the name itself.

Names also sometimes need to be changed. Children often go through periods of wanting to change their own names, which is why many parents give two or more names, so that the growing child may have a choice later in life.

Biblical stories frequently reflect this changing of names. For example, after he wrestled with the angel, Jacob's name changed to Israel, and he became the patriarch of the twelve tribes.

According to another story, the Jews enslaved in Egypt had become lax in their faith but were saved from total assimilation by maintaining two aspects that set them apart: they retained the custom of circumcision, and they held onto their Hebrew names. Finally, Proverbs 22 says, "A good name is rather to be chosen than good oil," oil in this case is a metaphor for wealth. "A good name" refers to reputation, but the underlying tradition holds to the concept that names are inherently valuable and powerful.

The Midrash teaches, "One should examine names carefully in order to give his child a name that is worthy so that they may become righteous, for sometimes the name is a contributing factor for good as for evil." Still, the power attributed to a "good" name is only as strong as the person who bears it. A good name is earned. The Mishnah, in the Talmud, tells us, "The crown of a good name excels all other crowns, including the crown of learning, of priesthood and even of royalty."

Long ago, naming involved the giving of only one name. And each child had an entirely unique name, belonging to no one else. In the period of the Bible, there is only one Abraham, one Isaac, Sarah, Solomon, with altogether 2,800 names, very few of which have been used in the twentieth century, though many of them have similarities to Native American names—for example, Deborah, "bee," and Tamar, which means "palm tree." Names that relate to nature have become popular again in recent decades in Israel—names such as Tal or Tali, which means "dew," and Elon or Elana, which means "oak."

Biblical Hebrew names have often been less popular than names from other languages and cultures, such as those from the Talmudic period, with Aramaic, Greek, and Roman names outnumbering biblical names among Jews. During the Middle Ages in eastern Europe, Jewish males were usually given both a secular name, called a Kinnui, and a religious name, a *shem leadosh*. Eventually, the secular name became so dominant that some

Shonna Husbands-Hankin.

parents didn't bother giving a Hebrew name, until the rabbis of the time decreed it mandatory to give one.

And so the tradition of having two names grew from this division of the secular and religious worlds. Names were selected very often by finding a direct translation of a Hebrew name, for example in Germany, the use of the first name Wolf was almost certainly based on the biblical name of Benjamin, whose tribe was associated with that animal, while in France, men called Chayim in the synagogue were often known as Vive on the street. However, originally and for a long time, boys got two names, whereas girls were given only one, sometimes a Hebrew name, such as Hannah or Rachel.

As the Jewish communities intermixed to a greater extent in different cultures and lands, and as the ghettos arose, so the Hebrew names changed and were replaced by less obvious Jewish names, so as to avoid recognition. Certain names became more popular among Jews, such as German names like Ludwig, Morritz, and Sigfried. Jewish immigrants to America selected less typical Jewish names and picked up Americanizations of their beloved past instead—such as the Yiddish name Blume (flower), which turned into Rose, Lily, and Iris. The old-country Tzvi (deer) who was known in Yiddish as Hersch (deer) became Harry.

In America Jewish people still use the secular and religious combination. A boy named after a relative called Moshe may be called to the Torah as Moshe, but his birth certificate will read Mark. A baby girl named after her grandmother Shayna may get the Hebrew name Shoshana and be called Susan by her friends. This form of assimilation begun long ago. In Ancient Greece, for example, men with the Hebrew name of Menachem commonly answered to Menaleus.

With the founding of the state of Israel in 1948, Hebrew became once again a modern language. Jewish names were enormously more popular. Those who settled in Palestine after the Holocaust chose to cast off reminders of the Diaspora, including certain names. Some Yiddish names were changed to Hebrew. Shayna (pretty one) became Yaffa, and Gittel (good one) became Tovah. Others chose Hebrew names that resembled some aspect of their existing names. Thus, Mendel and Morritz became Menachem and Meir.

The first generation of children born in Israel brought new names also, for example, Varda. Arnon (a stream bed), Kinereth (a sea), Barak (lightning) and Ora (light), were other new names. Ariella for a girl was born out of the boy's name Ariel, Gabriella after Gabriel. A few names were invented for both boys and girls: Yona (dove), Ayala and Ayal (deer), Leer and Leora (light) Liron and Lirona (song). Biblical names also reappeared after many generations of disappearance—Amnon, Yoram, Avital, Tamar.

So, for the naming of your new child, there is no lack of legend, tradition, and worth—a good name lasts forever, after all.

Brit Milah

Probably the most important reason why we continue to circumcise our boys is that to put an end to Brit Milah would be effectively, in most Jews' minds, to put an end to Jewish identity. Circumcision is not common only to the Jewish tradition, of course, but has been practiced by many cultures—in Egypt, Phoenicia, and much of modern America even today.

For Jews circumcision of the infant boy is a consecrated act and a religious obligation. It is, in effect, the covenant of Abraham—for Abraham obeyed God's command and circumcised himself—in his nineties, no less! The tradition today is to name a son at a circumcision on the eighth day after birth. This practice derives from Abraham's renaming at his Brit Milah. Isaac, the first son of a circumcised Hebrew, underwent Brit Milah on the eighth day, which is why the ritual has been performed eight days after birth ever since.

Brit Milah was already an ancient custom by the time the rabbis were writing the Talmud and Midrash, the books that explain and enlarge upon the Torah. The rabbinical literature includes many laws regulating the practice.

Brit milah is not performed on the eighth day simply because that was Isaac's age at his circumcision but because rabbinical wisdom holds that a child who has lived a seven full days has gained a measure of strength because he has had his first Shabbat. Further reasoning behind the eight days is that creation occurred in seven days and the eighth was the day when all was completed, and life began its process.

Essentially, Jews believe that the act of circumcision brings each individual closer to God, affirming the human ability to change.

In the Midrash the story is told that Adam was born without a foreskin, implying the lack of obstacles between him and God. The appearance of the foreskin in later generations was interpreted as a reminder of Adam's purity and the subsequent distance between men and God. Thus, tradition placed the day of Abraham's circumcision on the tenth of Tishri, the Day of Atonement when sins are forgiven.

The rabbis wrote that removing the foreskin was a way of sanctifying the act of procreation. This is in keeping with the Rabbinic attitude that every aspect of our life needs to be in alignment with God's will. For girls, it is becoming customary to have a *Brit Banot*, a naming ceremony, usually at home, during which a girl is entered into the covenant.

Circumcision Set, *Holland, 1827 & 1866.*
Jewish Museum, New York.

Chickpeas for Brit

Chickpeas are traditionally served at a bris. This recipe is a great accompaniment to any meal, and is beautiful, as well.

Sweet and Sour Chickpea Salad

6 TO 8 PORTIONS   PAREVE

¹/₂ cup high quality olive oil
1 cup finely minced onions (a sweet variety, if possible)
1 tbsp. each dried thyme and rosemary
¹/₂ each coarsely chopped red and yellow pepper
¹/₂ cup currents (raisins may be used)
4 cups chickpeas, drained and rinsed
        (either use canned or prepare dried chickpeas according to package directions)
¹/₂ tsp. salt
¹/₂ cup vinegar, either rice or white wine

Heat the oil in a saucepan. Add the onions and herbs and cook over low heat, for about 30 minutes. Add the peppers and cook for 5 minutes. Add the currents or raisins, cook for an additional 5 minutes.

Then add the chickpeas, stirring occasionally. Do not over-cook. Add salt, remove to a bowl and pour the vinegar over the hot mixture. Let the mixture cool, then cover and refrigerate overnight. Serve at room temperature.

This recipe doubles or triples very well. The amount of oil can be adjusted down when increasing the number of servings.

Shiva

The Jewish mourning rituals give us tools that lead us through the important steps in our sorrow from *Kriah* (brokenness) to *shalem* (wholeness).

Shiva draws family and friends together during the first week after a death. To truly mourn it is imperative that we allow our grief to come out, that we weep and remember the loved one. The Shiva period gives us a safe haven, a time, and space to fully mourn so that later we can move beyond it and heal. In lighting the *yahrzeit* candle a 24 hour candle of remembrance, we rekindle the memories we have of our family members on the anniversaries of their deaths.

The three periods of mourning after the death of a loved one are the first week the first month, and the first year. The first week is called Shiva and is observed by close relatives, who light a candle that remains lit for the whole seven days. the light symbolizing the presence of God in the house of mourning. Very often families remain at home and do not work during this time, and they recite the Kaddish each day.

People sit on the floor on low benches, cover their mirrors and refrain from wearing leather.

The practice of Shiva and the seven days of mourning dates back to biblical times. When Jacob died, his son Joseph mourned for seven days. The practice of sitting low derives from the story of Job when his whole family died. Friends came to his home and sat "beside him on the ground seven days and seven nights."

Traditionally mourners turn away from caring how they look during Shiva. Women stop wearing makeup, and men do not shave. Mirrors in the house of mourning are covered with cloth.

After the seven days are completed, the family or group of mourners go out for a walk and then return to the house as a symbol of their return to normal life again.

Kaddish, which is said daily during Shiva, is continued for 11 months. This is because it is held that even the worst individual will ascend to heaven if kaddish is recited for them for 12 months. Not to admit anything, but to hedge one's bet, the custom has become 11 months.

Reader's desk cover *by Belorussia Mogilev, 1871, velvet with silk and metal threads. Jewish Museum, New York.*

Sheloshim

The second period of mourning is called Sheloshim—the Hebrew word for "thirty"—and lasts for thirty days from the day of the funeral. This tradition is said to derive from the thirty days of mourning undertaken by the Israelites at the death of Moses.

Mourners return to work and school but the mourners do not attend social events and often go to the synagogue more frequently to recite the *Kaddish* prayer.

The Unveiling

The monument where the loved one has been buried is dedicated usually twelve months after the funeral. During this ceremony a cloth or veil covering the tombstone is lifted off and a brief prayer service is held during which the life of the individual is remembered and *Kaddish* is recited. This usually marks the end of the official mourning period.

Yahrzeit

Following the unveiling ceremony the mourners will of course continue to remember their loved one, so within the Jewish world there is an annual opportunity specially made for remembrance. The anniversary is called a *yahrzeit,* and each year of the Jewish calendar the family and friends recite the *Kaddish* and light a memorial candle which burns for twenty-four hours. Within the synagogue there can also be a special service called *Yizkor,* which means in Hebrew, "May God Remember." The *Yizkor* service also occurs during Passover, Shavuot, Sukkot, and Yom Kippur.

Bar Mitzvah/Bat Mitzvah

The Bar or Bat Mitzvah is the Jewish rite of passage from childhood to adulthood that occurs at the age of thirteen. *Mitzvot* are directives from God that provide the necessity and divinity of this time in a young boy or girl's life. This time is also one of initiation into the Jewish community as a responsible man or woman of duty, or son or daughter of the commandments.

Certain community responsibilities and privileges become a part of the individual's life at this stage, whether there is a formal Bar or Bat Mitzvah ceremony or not. The new adult is counted as a member of the *minyan*, the necessary quorum for prayer. He or she is eligible for an *Aliyah*, the privilege of being called to read from the Torah during services. By tradition the Bar or Bat Mitzvah is obliged to wear a *tallit*—a prayer shawl—or *tefillin* for morning prayers. In addition, fasting is required during Yom Kippur, and the oath of the individual is legally binding.

The Ceremony

At the Bar or Bat Mitzvah ceremony the thirteen-year-old is called to the Torah for the first time. It is a great honor for any Jewish individual to be invited to recite the blessings before and after the Torah is read. Known as an *Aliyah*—Hebrew for "going up"—the new adult goes up to the *Bimah*—the platform from which the Torah is read—and at that moment of initiation becomes a responsible adult Jew for the first time. Usually the reading is from the final section of the portion of the Torah, and the male who is so honored is called *Maftir* and the female *Maftirah*—from the Hebrew meaning "one who concludes." Following this reading, a piece from the biblical books of the prophets is chanted, called the *Haftarah*, which is taken from Isaiah, Jeremiah, or Ezekiel, depending on what portion of the Torah is read and what season of the year the service takes place.

During the time before the Bar or Bat Mitzvah ceremony, the boy or girl, through schooling and in attendance with the rabbi, learns the parts of the Torah and *Haftarah* that will be read. He or she may have to write a *d'var Torah,* and the "student" will be encouraged to participate in acts of *tzedakah*—helping those who are less fortunate.

Kaddish d'Rabbanan

BLESSING FOR THOSE WHO AIM TOWARD WISDOM
BY RABBI ARTHUR WASKOW

For the Godwrestlers of the people Yisrael
and for all who wrestle and who dance with God;

For our teachers the rabbis
and for the prophets, the poets, the shepherds, the builders,
the Redwoods and the rocks
for all our teachers;

For their students—including ourselves
and for the students of their students,
including those whom we go forth to teach;

For all who search deeply into Torah in its places
and all who aim their hearts and minds toward wisdom everywhere—

May there be
abundant love and kindness as we learn together
and flowing love that we carry from our learning
into our action in the world around us;
peace in our hearts
and a growing peace in the world around us;
an honorable and sufficient livelihood
that flows from working in harmony with earth;

And the blessing of awareness that all these blessings
come not from our isolated efforts
but from our weaving of our lives
as threads into the great web of all life
that is the Holy One.

Blessing the Fringes

A RITUAL FOR TZITZIT TYING AND
MAKING SACRED THE NEW OR RENEWED TALLIT
BY SHONNA HUSBANDS-HANKIN

The anticipation of an upcoming Bar or Bat Mitzvah, wedding, or older birthday often invites the gifting of a special new *tallit* (prayer shawl). As a silk *tallit* painter I found the opportunity presented itself to add further sacredness to the occasion by creating a ritual in which friends and relatives could join together in tying the special corner fringes *(tzitzit)* on the new

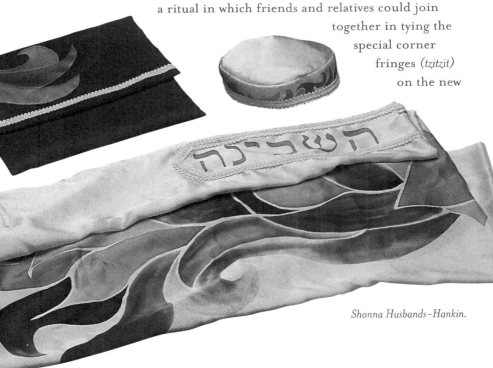

Shonna Husbands-Hankin.

or renewed *tallit* and blessing their loved one. Whether an occasion for women only or for both sexes, the basic ritual can be expanded and used in many settings.

My experience has been primarily with women only, oftentimes with a Bat Mitzvah girl and her friends and relatives. Usually the ritual is held the afternoon or evening one day before the Bat Mitzvah, when relatives have arrived. We gather in a bedroom, living room, or hotel room, sometimes lighting candles to create a nice atmosphere. Usually there is a fair amount of chaos in the room because relatives who haven't seen each other for a while are reconnecting, and usually almost no one has experienced creating a ritual. This is where the power of the event lies: in the tapping of the unconscious desire to make holy; in creating a format that embraces everyone where they are and that is brief and active enough that all feel engaged in doing something that really feels sacred.

For many people, especially the older women—the Great Aunt Suzies and Bubbe Rivkas and so forth—this ritual seems to activate and empower them to feel their spirituality and their womanness, making their Judaism accessible to them in a new way. Perhaps it is because many of them do not wear *tallitot* and have had their access to spirituality cut off from them, this ritual seems to awaken them deep within their being.

I have witnessed this reaction in all sorts of circles of polyester *bubbes* with gold-bangled jewelry who on the outside don't appear attracted to New Age Ritual. Yet on the inside many, perhaps most, are transformed by participating in a simple ritual that empowers a young woman of another generation to create a new, strong, vibrant, accessible, loving Judaism for herself.

Gathering in a circle around a table, we come together. We share reflections for a moment about the person we are there to honor, and I explain that we are going to tie the ritual fringes, or *tzitzit,* for the four corners of the *tallit.* With a wide spectrum of people participating, usually they are really chatty and it is hard to get the energy focused. So I spontaneously try to choose a song that might be familiar to most of them, like *Hene Ma Tov,* to engage them in singing together.

In tying the *tzitzit* we are wrapping and tying our love and blessing into the prayer shawl that will be carried forth in this person's life. The *tzitzit* have a special numerical value in the number of knots and twists and wraps, which symbolically add up to 613 (commandments/*Mitzvot*). The Ashkenazic and Sephardic methods of tying are slightly different. I use the Ashkenazic version with the sequence of 1 knot, 7 wraps, 1 knot, 8 wraps, 1 knot, 11 wraps, 1 knot, 13 wraps, final knot. We divide the group of people into four corners and rotate, taking turns tying and mapping each corner (the exact directions for tying *tzitzit* can be found in the first *Jewish Catalog*).

Kosher sets of *tzitzit* can be found in Jewish bookstores and gift shops for about three dollars. Sets of the blue threads *(techelet)* are available for about twenty dollars. And some women use red threads to wrap with from Rachel's *kever* or elsewhere as a symbolic gesture of prayer and connection with women's particular challenges. Some young girls like to bring small beads and charms to tie into the *tzitzit* to mark their personality and offering.

I am by no means an expert on any of this, let alone the kabbalistic meaning of the *tzitzit*. Others can share that piece of wisdom. I can only hope to guide you to create a beautiful and meaningful ceremony.

While we are tying, we do try to keep singing or humming a song to keep the energy in the room focused. When all four corners are complete, we bite off the excess length on the four long *shammash* threads, as no scissors or metal blades should be used on the *tzitzit*. Extra string is to be discarded by buying it, as with a holy book.

When the tying is completed, we all stand up and gather in a circle around the Bat Mitzvah girl. The *tallit* is folded up and passed around the circle. Each person is invited to make a brief blessing while holding the *tallit* in their hands. Some are silent in their turn. Many craft their own first blessings.

After the circle of sharing is complete, the *tallit* is opened up and held high above the girl, like a *chuppah*. We make a *She-he-heyanu* blessing together and sing one final song, wrapping the girl in her

Sukkot Decoration *from Montreal, 1950.*
Jewish Museum, New York.

tallit for the first time. We adjourn to cookies and juice, giggling, and laughter.

"Isn't it great that these girls just expect this ritual to happen for them now?" one mother of a local Bat Mitzvah said recently. "I never knew you could do something like this! When I was a girl…"

A great healing has taken place. A great transformation. With a sweet smile on everyone's face, the next day has new meaning. The *bubbes* and aunts and mothers are included now, in a new way. And the young sprout is empowered, and wrapped in love.

Ketubah, *Jewish marriage
contract from Iran, nineteenth century.
Haaretz Museum, Tel Aviv, Israel.*

100 Blessings a Day

BY JOHANNA "JHOS" J. SINGER

As part of their training for becoming Bat Mitzvah, I gave my students the assignment to choose a day of the coming week and make 100 blessings. This assignment originated from the Baal Shem Tov's advice that every Jew should make 100 blessings a day. One of my pupils, Shandra Kivel Luckey, kind of rolled her eyes and twisted a lock of green hair around one of her fingers and gave me that "Oh, Brother" look that has been perfected by twelve-year-olds worldwide, especially when they are relating to someone twenty-five years their senior. Still, she seemed somewhat intrigued by the assignment and nonchalantly asked a few questions about it—you know, Did the blessings have to be in Hebrew, Did they have to be only for Jewish things, and so on. I explained to the class that the idea of the homework was to notice all the ways in which their lives were blessed and that making 100 blessings would be so challenging that they would not have any energy to notice anything but blessing. This inspired the other look of disdain best offered by an adolescent: "Yeah right, Jhos—sigh." I noticed Shandra was scribbling something in her amazingly chaotic notebook. Sometime during the next week I swear the Baal Shem Tov was smiling, as I did, and as I continue to do when I read Shandra's 100 blessings.

SHANDRA'S BLESSINGS

These are the things I blessed today:

1. My comforter—for keeping me especially warm during the night.
2. My sheets—they keep my blankets clean.
3. My blanket—for keeping me cozy.
4. My clock—for sharing the time.
5. My dream—for waking me up.

6. My Guardian Mouse—for guarding me from nightmares.

7. My pajamas—for keeping me warm.

8. My pillows—for supporting my head.

9. My mattress—for supporting me while I sleep.

10. My shoes—so I don't have to look at the ground everywhere I walk.

11. My socks—who make my shoes comfortable.

12. My wardrobe—for giving me choice.

13. My cereal—Yummy!!

14. My strawberries—Super Yummy!!

15. The flowers in the front yard—they beautify the yard and attract birds, squirrels, insects, and people.

16. My lunchbox, for keeping my food together.

17. White picket fence, for keeping animals and such out and Abe in. [Abe is Shandra's ancient and much-beloved canine soul mate.]

18. My mom's car, for getting me to school on time.

Bereshit, *creation in ceramic tiles.*
Shonna Husbands-Hankin.

19. Streets and houses on the way to school, for being familiar.
20. My mom, for remembering my lunch.
21. Jamie, for greeting me nicely.
22. Jackie, because she is so hilarious and I love being with her.
23. Mrs. Streitfield, because she is a really good teacher and I learn a lot.
24. Todd, because he too is hilarious and incredibly entertaining.
25. My book, *Kindred Spirits*, a great book that expands my vocabulary.
26. My ears, because I would not learn so much, as easily, without them.
27. My feet, who supply transportation.
28. Lizzi, because she teaches me patience.
29. John, because he is nice and in my math group.
30. Ms. Miller, because she gave me a good math group.

31. My backpack, which helps me keep track of papers.
32. Ms. Davis, my first grade teacher who taught me how to read.
33. My water bottle, letting me get lots of water.
34. WATER, IT GIVES LIFE AND TASTES YUMMY!
35. Anna's ruler, which made this so much easier.
36. Bananas, Yummy and Healthful.
37. Dad, for buying challah.
38. Challah, for being yummy.
39. My locker, for keeping my stuff safe.
40. The pin, for keeping my locker open so I don't have to do the combo a lot.
41. Philly, because she will always give me a hug.
42. Daniel, because he knows when to stop.
43. Carpets, because they look and feel better than floors.
44. This pen, so I can write this down.
45. The moon, 'cause it is beautiful.
46. The sun, 'cause it gives life.
47. The soil, because it too gives life.
48. Trees, which are homes.
49. Color, for making things interesting.
50. Cartoons that make people laugh.
51. Walls, for dividing.
52. Doors, for giving me entrances.
53. Signs, for sharing helpful information.
54. Lips that speak.
55. Teeth that chew.
56. Livers and kidneys, because they get rid of poison.
57. My math book, for its kind service as a table.
58. Kleenex, so I can blow my nose without making a mess.
59. Stories that tell and entertain.
60. Shoelaces that keep shoes on.
61. Hair clips, because they keep hair out of my eyes.
62. Old sayings, because they teach.

63. Numbers, because they simplify things

64. Scissors that cut.

65. Bookmarks that keep places.

66. E-mail, because it makes communication easier.

67. Worms—make the earth fertile and richer.

68. Abe, because I love him.

69. Banks that keep my money safe.

70. Flashlights so I can see in the dark.

71. Books—the entrance to other worlds.

72. ELEPHANTS, because they ARE MAGNIFICENT.

73. Gymnastics, because it keeps me in shape.

74. Cats—even though they make me sneeze, they are a comfort to many people.

75. LAUGHTER—a medicine and a treasure.

76. Companionship, because it is necessary.

77. Microphones, so our voices are heard.

78. Cameras, to record our memories better.

79. Towels that dry.

80. Warmth, because it comforts, dries, and is necessary.

81. Blood—helps me live.

82. Incense, which scents the air with flavor.

83. Football—fun with friends; guys; and keeping my body in shape.

84. Lions—teach courage and bravery.

85. Paint—gives color and beauty.

86. Birth—the beginning of precious lives.

87. Art—gives perspective and understanding.

88. Sunsets—Beautiful Joys of Nature.

89. Guitar—helps me make music.

90. Cooperation—Holds it all together.

91. Rocks—History in physical form.

92. Crystals—wonders of nature.

93. Snow—beauty, water, destruction, and cold: 4 in 1!

94. Organization—gives order and it is easier to find things with it.

95. Homes, a special place to belong to. Necessary but not necessarily in one place.

96. Basketball—a great sport of physical exercise, teamwork, and fun.

97. Birthdays and holidays—just reasons to party!

98. Recycling—needed, and will delay the death of our world.

99. Wind to chill the spine, shake the trees, and comfort those on a hot day.

100. Death—the end, but needed to have a beginning. It is not evil, but to many people unwelcome, though it is as innocent as a flower.

Note: There are soooooooo many things that I did not get to mention, from dandelions to monkeys to soup to fossils and back again 1,001 times. 100 is a tiny number for this assignment, though it was time consuming. To me 100 was simplicity.

From puzzles to metal to architecture to tools to tents and cabins and back again, there are so many more blessings than 100.

From poems to conversations to relationships to whales to algae and back again—maybe I'm just good at this.

From cells to DNA to boxes to platypi, not to mention letters, summers, dew, clouds, instruments, and fog, and that was just 25 more from the top of my head...

Prayer before Torch Study

INTERPRETED BY NAOMI STEINBERG

In the narrowest sense Torah refers to the Five Books of Moses; in the broadest sense it encompasses the sum total of Jewish wisdom. Traditionally, the following blessing is said before Torah study. It is indeed uplifting to make this blessing before reading any Jewish material that uplifts, illumines, or inspires.

> *Baruch ata adonai eloneinu*
> *melech haolam asher kidshanu b'mitzvotav*
> *vitzivanu l'asok b'divrei torah.*

> *Blessed are You, Holy One, Source of Endless Time and Endless Space,*
> *who has made us whole with Your kind instructions, and instructed us to*
> *immerse ourselves in the words of Torah.*

Ethical Will

Upon the death of every Jew, his or her family and intimate friends may be left an inheritance set forth in three separate wills—the Will of Inheritance for money and belongings; the Living Will to instruct doctors and family on the procedures to be followed in case of terminal illness; and, finally, the Ethical Will, in which the person talks directly to those who will be left behind about hopes, dreams, and anything that should be cherished and passed on to future generations.

During the Middle Ages it was common practice for Jews to write Ethical Wills for their children and community. As one gets older and closer to death, there is often a desire to summarize one's life, to draw on the lessons learned, to share the insights gained over the years and with experience, and to leave behind one final message for future generations. For example, before he died, Jacob gathered his children and grandchildren around his bed and blessed them (Genesis 48-49), and Moses also offered a last blessing for each tribe of Israel before ascending to Mount Nebo to die (Deuteronomy 33). In the Talmud we also find many examples of Ethical Wills left by rabbis to their children. In recent years there has been a renewed interest in the practice of Ethical Wills: before we die we want to reflect on how we lived our lives and what legacies we leave to those we have lived with and loved, and we also want to express feelings of love, gratitude, grace, and blessing that will be received in letter form after we have left his world.

An Ethical Will is unique to the person who is writing it, there being no prerequisite format to follow. Some people want to share cherished memories of experiences that brought joy and light to the family; others leave suggestions for what kind of funeral or burial they want, what kind of music thay wish to be played at the ceremony, and a list of their favorite prayers and blessings that should be recited. Following are some of the traditional Jewish customs pertaining to burial and mourning that can be included in the Ethical Will.

- *K'ria* (in which mourners tear off their garments or ribbon actually or symbolically). Usually a fabric pinned to clothing and torn or actually torn clothing.

- Covering the mirrors in the house of mourning: this is a medieval superstition believed to safeguard the soul from becoming trapped by its own reflection on its way out of the body. Also to help mourners not be concerned with appearance.

- Mourners remain with the body from the moment of death until burial. Psalms are recited and talking is refrained from.

- *Taharah* (ritual washing of the body) usually by those who join a society for performing this *mitzvah*.

- Dressing the body in a shroud, a simple white garment.

- Wrapping the body in a *tallit* or shroud.

- Using a simple wooden coffin.

- Mourners shoveling dirt into the grave. Begun by those closest, this ritual makes the loss real, which assists in the mourning.

- Meal of consolation after the funeral.

- Observance of Shiva, the 7-day period of mourning during which family and friends gather each day, bring food and hold a *minyan* daily.

- Observance of Sheloshim, the 30-day mourning period following burial. Mourners return to normal life but avoid parties and the like.

One of the purposes of an Ethical Will is to examine our life and see where we may have fallen short, to define ourselves and ask for forgiveness - to make tshuvah - repentance.

In the act of dying it is good spiritual practice to review those areas of our lives and relationships in which we feel we have withheld love and compassion from our fellow human beings and ask for forgiveness.

Coffee service *from Staffordshire, England, 1769. Jewish Museum, New York.*

It is good spiritual practice to summarize one's life in an Ethical Will so that the most intimate people in our lives know how we truly felt about this journey. The summary may contain successes and failures, recollections of significant milestones, tender memories of loved ones. In summarizing our life for others we come to terms with its deeper meaning and destiny. In some sense we are trying to 'sum-up' so that those who come after us will have an easier time. The insights we bring to this Ethical Will becomes in the deepest way a true and touching gift for family and friends alike.

It is also appropriate to express thanks: to existence, to destiny, to those we love, and even to our enemies, if we are able to, who have also taught us valuable lessons. Expressing gratefulness is also an important spiritual practice.

Finally, an Ethical Will is a note from one generation to the next, perhaps it is a blessing, or a family tradition, or the description of a specific custom that bonds the members of your family in a unique way. Values are passed on from one generation to another, forming a long chain of tradition which is meant to only be a help.

> I am leaving you the fragrance of a Jerusalem morning...unforgettable perfume of thyme, sage, and rosemary that wafts down from the Judean hills. The heartbreaking sunsets that give way to Jerusalem at night...splashes of gold on black velvet darkness. The feel of Jerusalem stone, ancient and mellow, in the buildings that surround you....

> I am leaving you an extended family – the whole house of Israel. They are your people. They will celebrate with you in joy, grieve with you in sorrow....

> I am leaving you the faith of your forefathers... You have your heritage...written with the blood of your people through countless generations. Guard it well and cherish it – it is priceless!

–ETHICAL WILL OF DVORA WAYSMAN,
IN *WILLS: A MODERN JEWISH TREASURY*

COMING HOME

by Yehudit Steinberg-Caudill

I used to believe…
I had to run away from my roots & my heritage,
to find out who I really am.

and Now I realize that…
the journey in the desert is over.

"Coming Home" to my roots,
to receive my ancestors willingly
is the liberating force in Accepting Myself!!!

I celebrate the joy I feel deep inside of me.
I give thanks to the miracles of life,
and the courage to stand up to say;
"I Am Jewish and I Am Proud to Be!!!"

List of Contributors

Barry Barkan has learned about *rebbe* craft with Reb Zalman for twenty years. He is a founding member of the Aquarian Minyan of Berkeley and director of two organizations involved in program and community development and health care for elders. Founded the Live Oak Institute, an institution that has been working for twenty years to develop communities that heal the culture.

He can be contacted at:
Live Oak Institute
2150 Pyramid Drive
El Sobrante, California 94803.
Tel: 510-222-1242

Susan Duhan Felix is a pioneer in contemporary Jewish art, whose ceramics have been exhibited internationally from the Oakland Museum to Christie's in London, as well as being in permanent collections Listed in the 1993 *Who's Who In the World of Women,* nominated as the 1993 International Woman of the Year, she has been honored as an artist and activist by the State of California, and the City of Berkeley. Her ceremonial pieces represent the constant struggle to find light amidst the darkness of chaos of our lives.

She can be contacted at:
1436 Berkeley Way
Berkeley, California 94702.
Tel: 510-843-0588
Fax: 510-843-2730

Marcia Cohn Spiegel, M.A., is the founder of L'Chaim: 12 Steps to Recovery, helps people to create rituals of celebration and healing. She is co-author with Janet Carnay, Ruth Ann Magder, Laura Wine Paster, and Abigail Weinberg of *The Jewish Women's Awareness Guide: Connections for the Second Wave of Jewish Feminism* (New York: Biblio Press, 1992), and co-editor with Deborah Lipton Kremsdorf of *Women Speak to God: The Prayers and Poems of Jewish Women* (San Diego: Woman's Institute for Continuing Jewish Education, 1987).

She can be contacted at:
4856 Ferncreek Drive
Rolling Hills Estates, CA 90274
Tel: 310-378-3707
e-mail: mcspiegel@aol.com

or contact:
PROJECT KESHER,
1134 Judson Avenue
Evanson, IL 60202
Tel: 847-332-1994
Fax: 847-332-2134
e-mail: PROJECTKESHER@compuserve.com

Yitzhak Husbands-Hankin is the rabbi of Temple Beth Israel in Eugene, Oregon. He is also a cantor, performer, and composer of Jewish music.

Yitzhak Husbands-Hankin
Temple Beth Israel
42 W. 25th Avenue
Eugene, Oregon 97405
Tel: 541-485-7218

Shonna Husbands-Hankin is a Judaic artist in Eugene, Oregon. She creates wedding contracts *(ketubot)*, silk prayer shawls *(tallitot)*, wedding canopies *(chuppot)*, and other Jewish ritual objects. Shonna teaches Judaic art classes at Elat Chayyim, a Jewish retreat center in New York, and at Aleph Kallah and elsewhere. Her work is shown in art galleries and private collections all over North America. She is available for privately commissioned projects. Her writings appear in *Celebrating the New Moon: A Rosh Chodesh Anthology,* edited by Susan Berrin (Jason Aronson Publishers, 1996), *A Home for the Soul,* edited by Catherine Meyerowitz (Jason Aronson Publishers, 1995), and *Bat Mitzvah: A Jewish Girl's Coming of Age,* by Barbara Goldin (Viking, 1995).

Shonna Husbands-Hankin
90 W. 31st Avenue
Eugene, Oregon 97405
Tel: 541-484-6053
Fax: 541-343-2681

Daniel Lev, Ph.D., has served the San Francisco Bay Area over the last twenty-two years as Maggid. The word *maggid* comes from the Hebrew word that means "to relate, inform, tell." European maggidim would travel from town to town preaching and teaching Judaism, using stories. Differing from professional rabbis, contemporary North American maggidim spread Jewish spirituality and culture through the use of songs, stories, wild dancing, spiritual teachings, and experiential practices such as meditation and prayer. Their style is less formal and more intimate. Daniel Lev follows in this tradition. In addition, he holds a doctorate in clinical psychology and works with children families, and medical patients.

Daniel Lev, who considers himself a post-denominational Jew, tells stories and leads ecstatic singing in a variety of settings and loves to perform for everyone. He lives in the San Francisco Bay Area and can be reached at Tel: 510-845-2681.

Trisha Shendelman Margulies, born in Memphis, Tennessee, blends her years in Memphis, New York City, Los Angeles, and Chicago into a pate of tasteful textures. She has been a caterer and has taught Kosher cooking on both coasts. An avid reader of recipes, she shares her love of cooking with her mother and tests them on her four children and husband, who are her greatest beneficiaries and critics. Trisha currently resides in the Chicago area, spending much of her time volunteering for Hadassah. She can be reached at margulie@sprynet.com.

Rabbi Leah Novick is a counselor and spiritual teacher who draws on Jewish mystical tradition to guide her healing and ritual work. Reb Leah has been honored as "Pathfinder" by the Aleph Alliance for Jewish Renewal for her innovative contributions.

Monique Pasternak lives in Hawaii. She learns, teaches, writes, also devotes time and attention to some of the more intriguing happenings of life, as these continue to emerge. contact: melia@ilhawaii.net

Naomi Steinberg is a storyteller, poet, and folksinger, who serves as student rabbi for *B'nai Ha-Aretz* in rural northern California, where she has been active in the struggle to save the redwood forest. She sings with The Jewish Wedding Band and Noah's Dove.

Contact:
P.O. Box 274
Carlotta, CA 95528
e-mail: stein@humboldt1.com

Yehudit Steinberg-Caudill, M.Ed., is an arts and crafts activity designer for the Jewish Arts and Culture School in Berkeley, California, and is a Jewish creative-arts education specialist. Some of the projects she teaches include creating beeswax candles, *hallah* covers, and *Kiddish* cups for Sabbath, a menorah for Hannukah, masks and finger puppets for Purim, as well as hand-painted *talitot* and *kippah*. She also writes prayers and sacred poetry. She can be contacted by e-mail at: ecokosher1@aol.com

Rabbi Michael Strassfeld is an outstanding leader of services. He is one of the editors of the *Jewish Catalogues* and the author of *The Jewish Holidays,* editor of the forthcoming High Holiday Prayerbook of the reconstructionist movement. He is the rabbi of Congregation Ansche Chesed in New York City.

Arthur Waskow is director of the Shalom Center, fellow of Aleph—Alliance for Jewish Renewal, and author of *Godwrestling; Seasons of Our Joy; Down to Earth Judaism: Food, Money, Sex, and the Rest of Life;* as well as co-author of *Becoming Brothers.* From 1982 to 1989 he taught practical rabbinics at the Reconstructionist Rabbinical College.

Johanna J. Singer is a student rabbi and teacher at Chochmat HaLev in Berkeley. She can be reached through Chochmat at 510-704-9687 or Chochmat@best.com.

Judith Hankin is an artist whose company PomeGraphics produces cards and original papercut designs. Judith is also a talented artist producing Jewish ritual art. Contact: 345 Merry Lane, Eugene, OR 97405.

Kosher Foods

These are the overseeing organizations who guarantee that certain products are Kosher. Look for these symbols on packages. Kosher foods are either meat, milk, or pareve. Meat and milk may not be eaten together. Pareve may be eaten alone or with either meat or milk.

 Organized Kashrus Laboratories 1372 Carroll Street, Brooklyn, N.Y. 11213; Tel: 718-756-7500, Rabbi Dor Yoel Levy

 Tablet K 160-08 91st Street, Howard Beach, N.Y. 11414; Tel: 718-835-3595, Rabbi Rafael Saffra

 Orthodox Rabbinical Council of Greater Boston 611 Washington Street, Room 507, Boston, MA 02111 Tel: 617-426-9586, Rabbi Samuel J. Fox

 Square K 165 West 91 Street, New York, N.Y. 10024; Tel: 212-724-8663, Rabbi Harry Cohen,

Square K 5145 South Morgan Street, Seattle WA 98118; Tel: 206-723-3679, Rabbi Moshe Londinski

 "Star-K" Kosher Certification, 7504 Seven Mile Lane, Baltimore, MD 21208; Tel: (301) 484-4110, Rabbi Moshe Heinemann

Kashruth Supervision Service American Friends of Yeshivas Horav Bengis, 7111 Park Heights Avenue, Baltimore, MD 21215; Tel: 301-764-2735, Rabbi Shmuel Vitsick

 KOF-K Kosher Supervision 1444 Queen Anne Road, Teaneck, N.J. 07666; Tel: 20-837-0500, Rabbi Dr. H. Zecharia Senter

 Rabbi Yehudah Bukspan 6407 Orange Street, Los Angeles, CA 90048;Tel: 213-653-5083

 Kosher Overseers Associates of America, Inc. P.O. Box 1321, Beverly Hills, CA 90213; Tel: 213-870-0011, Rabbi Dr. Harold Sharfman

 The Union of Orthodox Jewish Congregations 45 West 36 Street, New York, N.Y. 10018; Tel: 212-564-9058, Rabbi Menachem Genack

 Vaad Harabonim (Vaad Hakashrus) of Mass. 177 Tremont Street, Boston, MA 02111; Tel: 617-426-6268, Rabbi Abraham Halbfinger

Names of God

So we may choose a name which resonates for us.

Adonai Lord
Ayla Force
Atika Kadisha Ancient Holy One
Av Harakhamim Father of Compassion, Merciful Father
Ayn Sof Infinite
Boray Creator
Ehyeh Asher Ehyeh I Will Be What I Will Be
Elohim Nature Power
El Elyon Most High God
El Ro-i God Who Sees Me
Go-elet Redeemer
Hakadosh Barukh Hu The Holy One Blessed Be He
Hakdosha B'rukha Hi The Holy One Blessed Be She
Hamakom The Space
Hashem The Name
Khay Ha-olamim Life Within All Worlds
M'kor Hakhayyim Source of Life
Malkah Queen
Mayan Raz Mysterious Well
Melekh King
Rachamayma Compassionate Womb Mother
Rakhamana Compassionate One
Rebonno Shel Olam Master of the Universe
Shaddai Almighty
Shalom
Shekhina Indwelling Presence
Tiferet Beauty
Tzur Rock
Yah
Yotzeret Form-Giver
Yesod Foundation

New Family Traditions

BY DR. STEVEN M. BROWN, HEADMASTER

SOLOMON SCHECHTER DAY SCHOOL OF PHILADELPHIA

The *berakhot* exemplified in this calendar form a rich backdrop for everyday family living imbued with Jewish values and activities. The following family activities may help expand and enhance the importance of these *berakhot*.

Asher Natan Lesekhvi Vinah In reaction to the morning *berakhot*, and to help your family feel God's loving presence, keep a family list prominently posted, beginning with the phrase "God is when..." Complete with examples such as when we do a *mitzvah,* experience wonder, feel love, help someone in need, etc.

Sheheheyanu Review your family picture album or videotapes to see where reciting the *Sheheheyanu* would have been appropriate. Add this *berakhot* to the album page or do a voice-over on the video.

La'asok B'divrei Torah To exemplify daily "busying ourselves with Torah," create a list of carpool questions on the personalities of biblical figures, problems of good and evil in the world, questions about God, or ethical dilemmas from Jewish tradition that can stimulate Torah discussion and study while driving with a group of energetic youngsters.

Birkat Ha'gomel Watch the evening news or review the front page of the daily newspaper and invite family members to suggest individuals who ought to be saying *Birkat Ha'gomel.*

Ha'motzi Lehem Min Ha'aretz List or illustrate the detailed chain of people (including the truck drivers, farm machinery repair persons, and financiers) involved in bringing a loaf of bread to the family table. Post the illustrated step-by-step process for all to see and remember when saying the *berakhah.*

Birkat Ha'brit Acquire (or make) a family *hallah* cover on which are embroidered the names of all present family members. Add new names (babies and future spouses) as they accrue. Use this cover at the *seudat mitzvah* of a *brit* or *simhat bat* celebration.

Barukh Hakham Ha'razim Make a family collage titled with this *berakhah*. Record the results of a family brainstorming session, listing the strengths and specialness of each member. List the results around members' portraits.

Shekoho U'gvurato To cultivate a deeper sense of the awe and wonder of the universe in family members, complete these phrases: I wonder if…; I wonder about…; I wonder why…; I wonder how…; I wonder whether…; I wonder when…; or, since thunder is frightening to many, discuss how saying a *berakhah* in reaction to thunder can change a moment of fear to one of appreciation for the fact that nature is working properly.

Ha'mapil Hevlei Sheinah Photocopy and enlarge this *berakhah* in Hebrew and in English. Invite children to decorate it with calming, familiar items they would like to think about at bedtime. Laminate the paper and affix it somewhere near your child's bed to be used each night.

Dayyan Ha'emet Help family members cope with difficult moments by familiarizing them with the formula, "May God comfort you among all the mourners of Zion and Jerusalem," to be said when departing from a *shiva* house and taking leave of the mourner.

Zokher Ha'brit Make a family covenant or contract outlining mutual obligations, responsibilities, and privileges. Decorate with a rainbow and sign, making each letter of your name a different color. Post prominently in your household.

Shekakhah Lo B'olamo Prepare a banner of this *berakhah* for your *sukkah*. During the year, gather appropriate pictures of nature's beauty from magazines and newspapers; affix to banner, laminate, and hang; or, since this *berakhah* is often said upon seeing beautiful creatures in nature, ask family members to consider the following questions: Which animal do I like best? How am I most like this animal? How would I like to be more like this animal? Act it out.

Birkat Ha'l'vanah Monthly, before the moon wanes, go outside, recite *Birkat Ha'l'vanah* and recount stories of Jewish heroines throughout the ages to reflect the feminine presence in our lives.

Keeping the Flame Alive:
A LIST OF SCHOOLS AND CENTERS

Following is a list of schools, centers, and retreat sanctuaries that either teach Jewish spirituality and ritual or network with Jewish communities nationally. Several offer retreats and weekly classes. Some focus on text study and adopt a more orthodox approach to Judaism. We suggest that you contact one nearest to you and ask for their program and details of how you can enroll. We suggest that you take the plunge and attend one or two classes as soon as possible to get a flavor of meditation and put to practice some of the principles discussed in the book. You will find the directors and staff of all the centers listed here very helpful and welcoming of new students.

Chochmat HaLev

Co-directors: Avram Davis, Ph.D., and Nan Fink Ph.D.

2525 8th Street #13
Berkeley, CA 94710
Tel: 510-704-9687
Fax: 510-704-1767
e-mail: chochmat@best.com

Specializing in extended teaching of meditation and Jewish spirituality. Sends teachers to other national centers and trains teachers in meditation and aspects of Jewish spirituality. Organizes meditation sitting groups nationally, conducts retreats, and offers guided text study.

Ruach Ami: Bay Area Jewish Healing Center (BAJHC)

3330 Geary Boulevard
3rd Floor West
San Francisco, CA 94118
Tel: 415-750-4197
Fax: 415-750-4115

Rabbi Miriam Senturia,
Rabbi Jeffrey Silberman,
and/or Rabbi Eric Weiss

For Jews living with illness, their loved ones, and the bereaved. Services include pastoral counseling, spiritual support groups, healing prayer services, information, and referral.

Metivta
Director: Rabbi Jonathon
Omer-Man

2001 S. Barrington Avenue #106
Los Angeles, CA 90025
Tel: 310-477-5370

A center with emphasis on meditation training. Trains teachers.
Conducts meditation retreats.

Heart of Stillness Hermitage
Directors: Rabbi David Cooper
and Shoshanna Cooper

PO Box 106
Jamestown, CO 80455
Tel: 303-459-3431

Teaches meditation nationally.
Specializes in sustained silent
retreats.

Yakar
Director: David Zeller

10 HaLamed Hay Street
Jerusalem 93361
Tel: 011-972-2-612310

A center with orthodox perspective. Emphasis on general Jewish
spirituality and text study.
Teaches meditation.

Gershon Winkler
PO Box 1865
Cuba, NM 87013
Tel: 505-289-3620

This is a remote retreat with space
for just a few people. Gershon
Winkler is a teacher in Jewish
Shamanistic path who gives an
irreverent but high level of
teaching.

Academy for Jewish Learning
Director: Shohamma Weiner

15 West 86th Street
New York, NY 10024
Tel: 212-875-0540

This is a general-purpose semi-
nary in which different aspects of
Judaism can be studied. There is
some emphasis on spirituality.

**Aleph—Alliance for Jewish
Renewal and Network for Jewish
Renewal Communities**
Director: Daniel Siegel

7318 Germantown Avenue
Philadelphia, PA 19119-1793
Tel: 215-247-9700
e-mail: ALEPHAJR@aol.com

Conducts a biannual national
conference with large selection
of classes and opportunities
for creating Jewish spiritual
communities.

**Elat Chayyim: A Center
for Healing and Renewal**
Directors: Jeff Roth
and Joanna Katz

99 Mill Hook Road
Accord, NY 12404
Tel: 1-800-398-2630

This is a retreat center, offering
an innovative program. It provides
a cross selection of classes and
subjects on Jewish spirituality.

**Congregation led by Rabbi
Lawrence Kushner**
Beth El
105 Hudson Road
Sudbury, MA 01766
Tel: 508-443-9622

National Havurah Committee
7318 Germantown Avenue
Philadelphia, PA 19119-1793
Tel: 215-248-9760
e-mail:
73073.601@compuserve.com

A committee for supporting and
expanding Havurot communities.
Also organizes a yearly national
conference.

**United Synagogues of
Conservative Judaism**
Rapaport House
155 Fifth Avenue
New York, NY 10010
Tel: 212-533-7800
e-mail: www.Uscj.org

Union of Orthodox Congregations
333 Seventh Avenue, 18th Floor
New York, NY 10001
Tel: 212-563-4000

Jewish Women International
8323 Southwest Freeway,
Suite 385
Houston, TX 77074
Tel: 1-800-891-4243
and 415-756-1436

A strong voice for the effectiveness
of Jewish women, the emotional
well-being of children, and
strengthening of Jewish life and
values. Advocates for contemporary issues: interfaith families,
domestic violence, and prejudice
reduction. An independent,
self-governing Jewish women's
organization, taking action on
local, national, and international
levels.

**Union of American
Hebrew Congregations
(UAHC Reform)**
838 Fifth Avenue
New York, NY 10021-7064
Tel: 212-650-4000
e-mail: uahc@uahc.org
web site: www.uahcweb.org

**Jewish Reconstructionist
Federation**
1299 Church Road
Wyncote, PA 19095-1898
Tel: 215-887-1988
Fax: 215-887-5348

Interfaith Connection
Director: Roseanne Levitt
JCC of San Francisco
3200 California Street
San Francisco, CA 94118
Tel: 415-292-1252
Fax: 415-346-4556

**Jewish Community Information
and Referral (JCI&R)**
Director: Gail Green

Jewish Community Federation
121 Steuart Street
San Francisco, CA 94105
Tel: 415-777-0411
Fax: 415-777-4545
e-mail: sfjcir@cjf.noli.com

Bibliography

Becher, Itzik. *Living Traditions.* Toronto: Doubleday Canada, 1993.

Diamant, Anita. *The New Jewish Baby Book.* Woodstock, VT: Jewish Lights, 1993.

——— . *The Jewish Wedding.* New York: Summit Books, 1985.

Epstein, Morris. *All About Jewish Holidays and Customs.* Hoboken, NJ: Ktav Publishing House, 1970.

Hammerschlag, Carl A., and Howard D. Silverman. *Healing Ceremonies.* New York: Putnam Berkeley Publishing Group, 1997.

Harlow, Jules, Rabbi, ed. *Siddur Sim Shalom—A Prayerbook for Shabbat, Festivals, and Weekdays.* New York: Rabbinical Assembly of the United States of America, 1985.

——— . *A Rabbi's Manual.* New York: Rabbinical Assembly of the United States of America, 1965.

Hays, Edward. *Prayers for the Domestic Church.* Leavenworth, KS: Forest of Peace Books, 1979.

——— . *Prayers for a Planetary Pilgrim.* Leavenworth, KS: Forest of Peace Books, 1989.

Imber-Black, Evan, and Janine Roberts. *Rituals for Our Times.* New York: HarperCollins, 1992.

Kushner, Lawrence. *Honey from the Rock.* Woodstock, VT: Jewish Lights, 1994.

Pasternak, Monique. *Like a Deer Upon the Mountains.* Fort Bragg, CA: Ocean Star Publications, 1991.

——— . *Flying on the Wings of Aleph.* Fort Bragg, CA: Ocean Star Publications, 1988.

Shiovitz, Jeffrey, Cantor. *B'kol Echad—In One Voice.* New York: United Synagogue of Conservative Judaism, Dept. of Youth Activities, 1995.

Siegel, Richard, Michael Strassfeld, and Sharon Strassfeld, eds. *The First Jewish Catalog.* Philadelphia: Jewish Publication Society of America.

Stern, Chaim, ed. *On the Doorposts of Your House.* New York: Central Conference of American Rabbis, 1994.

Strassfeld, Michael. *The Jewish Holidays.* New York: Harper & Row, 1985. *The New Jewish Catalog: A Spiritual Guide,* Shocken.

United Jewish Appeal. *Book of Songs and Blessings.* United Jewish Appeal. 1993.

Wiener, Harris, Shohama Omer-Man, and Jonathan Omer-Man, eds. *Worlds of Jewish Prayer.* Northvale, NJ: Jason Aronson, 1993.

Additional Readings

Becher, Itzik. *Living Traditions.* Toronto: Doubleday Canada, 1993.

Davis, Avram, ed. *Meditation from the Heart of Judaism: Today's Masters Teach about Their Practice, Discipline, and Faith.* Woodstock, VT: Jewish Lights, 1997.

Davis, Avram, and Manuela Dunn-Mascetti. *Judaic Mysticism.* New York: Hyperion, 1997.

Diamant, Anita. *The New Jewish Baby Book.* Woodstock, VT: Jewish Lights, 1993.

——— . *The Jewish Wedding.* New York: Summit Books, 1985.

Epstein, Morris. *All About Jewish Holidays and Customs.* Hoboken, NJ: Ktav Publishing House, 1970.

Falk, M. *The Book of Blessings.* San Francisco: Harper, 1996.

Hammerschlag, Carl A., and Howard D. Silverman. *Healing Ceremonies.* New York: Putnam Berkeley Publishing Group, 1997.

Harlow, Jules, Rabbi, ed. *Siddur Sim Shalom—A Prayerbook for Shabbat, Festivals, and Weekdays.* New York: Rabbinical Assembly of the United States of America, 1985.

——— . *A Rabbi's Manual.* New York: Rabbinical Assembly of the United States of America, 1965.

Hays, Edward. *Prayers for the Domestic Church.* Leavenworth, KS: Forest of Peace Books, 1979.

——— . *Prayers for a Planetary Pilgrim*. Leavenworth, KS: Forest of Peace Books, 1989.

Imber-Black, Evan, and Janine Roberts. *Rituals for Our Times*. New York: Harper Collins, 1992.

Kushner, L. *Honey from the Rock*. Woodstock, VT: Jewish Lights, 1994.

——— . *The River of Light*. Woodstock, VT: Jewish Lights, 1990.

——— . *The Book of Words*. Woodstock, VT: Jewish Lights, 1993.

Pasternak, Monique. *Like a Deer Upon the Mountains*. Fort Bragg, CA: Ocean Star Publications, 1991.

——— . *Flying on the Wings of Aleph*. Fort Bragg, CA: Ocean Star Publications, 1988.

Shiovitz, Jeffrey, Cantor. *B'kol Echad—In One Voice*. New York: United Synagogue of Conservative Judaism, Dept. of Youth Activities, 1995.

Siegel, Richard, Michael Strassfeld, and Sharon Strassfeld, eds. *The First Jewish Catalog*. Philadelphia: Jewish Publication Society of America.

Stern, Chaim, ed. *On the Doorposts of Your House*. New York: Central Conference of American Rabbis, 1994.

Strassfeld, Michael. *The Jewish Holidays*. New York: Harper & Row, 1985.

United Jewish Appeal. *Book of Songs and Blessings*. United Jewish Appeal, 1993.

Wiener, Harris, Shohama Omer-Man, and Jonathan Omer-Man, eds. *Worlds of Jewish Prayer*. Northvale, NJ: Jason Aronson, 1993.

Winkler, G., and Lakme Batya Elior. *The Place Where You Are Standing Is Holy*. Northvale, NJ, Jason Aronson, 1994.

Readings for Jewish Spiritual Practice

Following is a list of books we recommend as the fundamentals for inspiring and informing your spiritual practice.

Penina Adelman. *Miriam's Well*. Biblio Press, 1990.
A guide to women's celebration of Rosh Hodesh throughout the year. Good ideas for meditation.

Allen Afterman. *Kabbalah and Consciousness*. Sheep Meadow Press, 1992.
A review of the Jewish mystical tradition, with an emphasis on the impact of the kabbalah on modern consciousness.

Bradley Artson. *It's a Mitzvah! Step-by-Step to Jewish Living*. Behrman House, 1996.

Yitzhak Buxbaum. *Jewish Spiritual Practices*. Aronson, 1990.
Comprehensive guidebook to the spiritual dimension of the Halachic behavior and Jewish living. Many suggestions for deepening practice.

David A. Cooper. *Silence, Simplicity, and Solitude*. Bell Tower, 1992. Guide for spiritual retreat.

Avram Davis. *The Way of Flame*. HarperCollins, 1996.
A guide to the mystical path of Judaism, a path of heart and soul.

——— , ed. *Meditation from the Heart of Judaism: Today's Masters Teach about Their Practice, Discipline, and Faith*. Jewish Lights, 1997.
A complete compendium of spiritual teachers, practices, disciplines, and faith.

Avram Davis and Manuela Dunn-Mascetti. *Judaic Mysticism*. Hyperion, 1997.
An introduction to mystical Judaism, spiritual practices, and meditation.

Hayim Halevy Donin. *To Pray As a Jew*. Basic Books, 1980.
Written by an orthodox rabbi, this book goes through the service, giving historical information and suggestions of meaning.

Perle Epstein. Kabbalah: *The Way of the Jewish Mystic*. Shambhala, 1988.
This study traces the history of the kabbalah and unravels the web of
ancient traditions hidden in texts. Good introductory book

Steven Fisdell. *The Practice of the Kabbalah*. Aronson, 1996.
Step-by-step exploration into the realm of kabbalistic meditation.

Evelyn Garfield. *Service of the Heart*. Aronson, 1994.
Introduction to the *Siddhur*, informative commentary.

Lynn Gottlieb. *She Who Dwells Within*. HarperCollins, 1995.
Feminist prayers, guided meditations, and rituals.

Daniel Gordis. *God Was Not in the Fire: The Search for a Spiritual Judaism.*
Ideas on deepening Jewish understanding and practice.

Joel Lurie Grishaver. *And You Shall Be a Blessing*. Aronson, 1993
An exploration of the six words that begin every traditional *Brachah*.

Reuven Hammer. *Entering Jewish Prayer*. Schocken Books, 1994
Another good commentary on Jewish prayer.

Edward Hoffman. *The Way of Splendor: Jewish Mysticism and Modern Psychology.*
Aronson, 1992.
A good introduction to Jewish mysticism, exploring the relationship
between the mystical tradition and the teachings of modern psychology.

Aryeh Kaplan. *Jewish Meditation*. Schocken Books, 1985.
A practical guide to meditation, written by an orthodox rabbi well versed
in the Kabbalah. Helpful ideas for a spiritual practice.

Lawrence LeShan. *How to Meditate*. Bantam Books, 1974.
Guide to generic meditation, first steps.

Kerry Olitzky. *100 Blessings Every Day*. Jewish Lights, 1993.
Exercises for personal growth and renewal throughout the Jewish year.

Ellen Umansky and Dianne Ashton. *Four Centuries of Jewish Women's Spirituality.*
Beacon, 1992.
A sourcebook of spirituality as seen through the eyes of women. Lots of
archival material.

Acknowledgments

Sara Shendelman and Avram Davis would like to thank the following persons for their contributions to the book: Philip and Manuela Dunn for their patience and hard work in making this complex subject work so well in one small book. The wonderful designers Renee Harcourt, and Janet Mumford of i4 Design in Sausalito, and Laurie Abkemeier at Hyperion for her careful and watchful eye. Also our heartfelt thanks to Rabbi Arie Becker, Dr. Daniel Thursz, and to the parents of Sara Shendelman, George and Esther Shendelman.

Grateful acknowledgment is made for permission to reproduce the following material: the recipes found throughout *Part I: The Holiday Cycle*, © Trisha Shendelman Margulies are printed here by kind permission of the author. The piece on arts and crafts for Rosh ha-Shanah on page 30, © Judith Hankin is printed here by kind permission of the artist. *Yom Kippur Story* on pp. 47-49, *Real Hanukkah Stories* on pp. 86-88, *Purim Story* on pp. 101-102, *Shavuot Story* on pp. 128-129, *Tisha Be-Av Story* on pp. 132-134, and *Shabbat Story* on pp. 150-152, traditional Jewish stories retold by Daniel Lev, © Daniel Lev are reprinted here by kind permission of the author. The story on pp. 138-139, is originally found in *A Festschrift in Honor of Zalman Schachter-Shalomi*, edited by Shohama Wiener and Jonathan Omer-Man, and reproduced here by kind permission of Jason Aaronson Publishers. *Shabbat Candlemaking* on page 153, *Creating a Women's Rosh Chodesh Ceremony* on pp. 181-191 and *Turned My Mourning Into Dancing* on page 194, and *Coming Home* on page 226, © Yehudit Steinberg-Caudill are printed here by kind permission of the author. The *Nishmat* prayer on page 154 and *Kaddish d'Rabbanan* on page 209, © Rabbi Arthur Waskow are reproduced by kind permission of the author. *The Dream— A Reading—Aloud Story for Havdallah* on pp. 156-157, *Bedtime Prayers* on page 175, and *Prayer Before Torah Study* on page 221, © Naomi Steinberg are printed here by kind permission of the author. *The Power of Blessing* on pp. 159-161 and *Some Guiding Concepts for Derek Habrachot—The Blessing Path* on pp. 162-163, © Jonathan Omer-Man and Shohama Wiener are reprinted here by kind permission of the authors. *The Simcha Cup* on pp. 164-166, *An Artist's Blessing* on pp. 167-169, and *Blessing the Fringes* on pp. 210-213, © Shonna Husbands-Hankin are printed here by kind permission of the author. *The Prayer For Healing Through Medicine* on page 174, © Yitzhak Husbands-Hankin is printed here by kind permission of the author. *The Blessing for Invoking Celestial Guides* on pp. 174-175, © Rabbi Leah Novick is printed here by kind permission of the author. *Creating Our Own Blessing* on pp. 176-178 and *Old Symbols, New Rituals* on pp. 179-180, © Marcia Cohn Spiegel are printed here by kind permission of the author. *100 Blessings a Day* on pp. 215-220, © Johanna J. Singer is printed here by kind permission of the author.

Art Acknowledgments

Jacket Front: Omer Calendar by Georges Goldstein. Jewish Museum, New York.
Jacket Back: Shiviti, Jewish Museum, New York

Jewish Museum/Art Resource, New York: page 7: *The Wedding* by Leo Schatzman;
page 11: presentation plate made by Josef Mitterbacher; page 12: Wedding ring;
page 20: Illuminated manuscript from a German Haggadah; pages 24-25:
Shofar from Russia, 19th century; page 26: Rosh ha-Shanah plate; page 29:
Jewish New Year banner; page 41: Sabbath cloth from Iran; pages 42-43:
Mizrah; pages 48-49: Sabbath candlesticks from Russia; page 52: Sukkot decoration; page 56: Etrog container; page 59: Etrog container; pages 64-65:
Megillah; pages 66-67: Mizrach; page 70: Hanukkah lamp; page 71: North
African Hanukkah lamp; pages 72-73: Hanukkah lamp; page 75: Spinning tops
for Hanukkah game; page 76: Hanukkah lamp in the form of the Ark; page 82:
Hanukkah greeting card; page 94: Purim rattlers; page 95: Purim cup; pages
96-97: Purim grogger; page 100: Purim cup; pages 102-103: Purim painting;
page 104: Zinc plate; pages 106-107: Ceramic Passover plate; page 108: Seder
towel; page 111: Seder plate; page 114: Kiddush cup; page 119: Matzah bag;
page 122: Mazatah bag; page 130: Charity cup; page 132-133: Seder plate; pages
134-135: Charity boxes; page 142: Spice container; pages 146-147: The Scroll
of Esther; page 155: Kiddush cup; pages 160-161: Scroll of Esther; page 165:
Kiddush cup; page 177: The Scroll of Esther; page 179: Skull cap and belt;
pages 184-185: Seven-branched candelabrum; page 192: Marriage contract;
page 200: Circumcision plate; page 201: Circumcision set; pages 204-205:
Reader's desk cover; page 207: Megillah and case; page 208: Megillah and case;
page 213: Sukkot decoration; pages 220-221; Megillah Esther Scroll; page 224:
Coffee service.

© **Judith Hankin**: page 9: *Deer in the Field*; page 23; page 30: *Like an Apple Tree*; page
55; page 69: *Recieving the Torah*; page 79; page 87; page 112; page 126; page 141;
page 157; page 170: *I Went Down to the Nut Garden*; page 175; page 181; pages 182-183.

© **Shonna Husbands-Hankin**: page 16; page 39; pages 50-51; page 89; page 92;
page 121; page 125; page 144; page 151; pages 162-163; page 167; page 173;
pages 188-189; page 197; page 210; pages 216-217.

Erich Lessing Collection from Art Resource, New York: page 105: Passover feast; page
116: Seder plate; page 131: Mizrach decoration; page 136: Megillah; pages 138-
139: Shviti; page 168: Ketubah; page 214: Ketubah.

© **Sara Shendelman and Avram Davis**: page 112; page 167; page 175

© **Miriam Stampfer**: page 158: *Counting of the Omer*.

© **Susan Felix**: pages 34-35: *Blessing Bowl*; pp. 203 & 207: *Yahrzeit Candle*

Baruch Atah Adonai Elohaynu Melech
HaOlam Sheh'asah Nisim La'Avotaynu
BaYamim HaHaym BaZ'man HaZeh

Blessed is the Eternal our God,
Sovereign of the universe, who
performed miracles for our
ancestors in days of old, at this
season.

Presach

For the blessing over wine, see
Shabbat.

Baruch Atah Adonai Elohaynu Melech
HaOlam, Boray P'ri HaAdamah

Blessed is the Eternal our God,
sovereign of the universe, Creator
of the fruit of the earth. (Karpas)

Baruch Atah Adonai Elohaynu Melech
HaOlam Asher Kid'shanu b'Mitzvotav
v'Tzivanu Al Achilat Maror.

Blessed is the Eternal our god,
Sovereign of the universe, who
sanctifies us through Your commandments and commands us
concerning the eating of bitter
herbs.

Baruch Atah Adonai Elohaynu Melech
HaOlam Asher Kid'shanu b'Mitzvotav
v'Tsuvanu Al Achilat Matzah.

Blessed is the Eternal our God,
Sovereign of the universe, who
sanctifies us through Your commandments and commands us
concerning the eating of matzah.

For the blessing over bread, see
Shabbat.

Baruch Atah Adonai Elohaynu Melech
HaOlam Asher Kid'shanu b'Mitzvotav
v'Tsuvanu Al Netilat Yadayim.

Blessed is the Eternal our God,
Sovereign of the universe, who
sanctifies us through Your commandments and commands us
concerning the washing of hands.

Candlelighting for a Festival

Baruch Atah Adonai Elohaynu Melech
HaOlam Asher Kid'shanu b'Mitzvotav
v'Tsuvanu l'Hadleek Nayr Shel (Shabbat
v'Shel) Yom Tov.

Blessed is the Eternal our God,
Sovereign of the universe, who
sanctifies us through Your commandments and commands us to
kindle the (Shabbat and) Festival
lights.

Baruch Atah Adonai Elohaynu Melech
HaOlam Shehecheyanu v'Keeyamanu
v'Higeeyanu LaZ'man HaZeh.

Blessed is the Eternal our God,
Sovereign of the universe, who has
kept us alive, watched over us, and
enabled us to reach this season.

Baruch Atah Adonai Elohaynu Melech
HaOlam Boray P'ri HaAytz.

Blessed is the Eternal our God,
Sovereign of the universe, who
creates the fruits of the tree.

Yehi Ratzon Milfanecha Adonai Elohaynu
Vaylohay Avotaynu Sheh'the'chadaysh
Alaynu Shanah Tovah u'Metukah.

May it be Your will, O Eternal

our God and God of our ancestors, that You renew us for a good and sweet year.

Sukkot

Baruch Atah Adonai Elohaynu Melech HaOlam Asher Kid'shanu b'Mitzvotav v'Tzivanu Layshayv BaSukkah.

Blessed is the Eternal our God, Sovereign of the universe, who sanctifies us through Your commandments and commands us to dwell in the sukkah.

Baruch Atah Adonai Elohaynu Melech HaOlam Asher Kid'shanu b'Mitzvotav v'Tzivanu Al Netilat Lulav.

Blessed is the Eternal our God, Sovereign of the universe, who sanctifies us through Your commandments and commands us concerning lifting up the lulav.

Chanukah

Baruch Atah Adonai Elohaynu Melech HaOlam Asher Kid'shanu b'Mitzvotav v'Tzivanu l'Hadleek Nayr Shel Chanukah.

Blessed is the Eternal our God, Sovereign of the universe, who sanctifies us through Your commandments and commands us to kindle the Chanukah lights.

Baruch Atah Adonai Elohaynu Melech HaOlam Sheh'asah Nisim La'Avotaynu BaYamim HaHaym BaZ'man HaZeh.

Blessed is the Eternal our God, Sovereign of the universe, who performed miracles for our ancestors in days of old, at this season.

Purim

Baruch Atah Adonai Elohaynu Melech HaOlam Asher Kid'shanu b'Mitzvotav v'Tzivanu Al Mikra Megillah.

Blessed is the Eternal our God, Sovereign of the universe, who sanctifies us through Your commandments and commands us to read the Megillah.

Shabbat

Baruch Atah Adonai Elohaynu Melech HaOlam Asher Kid'shanu b'Mitzvotav v'Tzivanu L'hadleck Nayr Shel Shabbat.

Blessed is the Eternal our God, Sovereign of the universe, who sanctifies us through Your commandments and commands us to kindle the Sabbath lights.

Baruch Atah Adonai Elohaynu Melech HaOlam Boray P'ri HaGefen.

Blessed is the Eternal our God, Sovereign of the universe, Creator of the fruit of the vine.

Baruch Atah Adonai Elohaynu Melech HaOlam HaMotzi Lechem Min HaAretz.

Blessed is the Eternal our God, Sovereign of the universe, who brings forth bread from the earth.

Y'simcha Elohim k'Ephraim v'chi Menasheh.

May God make you as Ephraim and as Menasseh.

CIVIL CALENDAR — **HEBREW CALENDAR**

1999   **5759**

	SUN	MON	TUE	WED	THU	FRI	SAT		SUN	MON	TUE	WED	THU	FRI	SAT	SABBATH	
JANUARY	27	28	29	30	31	1	2	⟷	8	9	10 Fast Tebeth	11	12	13	14	Vayhi	TEBETH
	3	4	5	6	7	8	9	⟷	15	16	17	18	19	20	21	Shemoth	
	10	11	12	13	14	15	16	⟷	22	23	24	25	26	27	28	Vaera*	
	17	18	19	20	21	22	23	⟷	29	1	2	3	4	5	6	Bo	
	24	25	26	27	28	29	30	⟷	7	8	9	10	11	12	13	Beshallah Shirah	SHEBAT
	31	1	2	3	4	5	6	⟷	14	15 Ham. Asar	16	17	18	19	20	Yithro	
FEBRUARY	7	8	9	10	11	12	13	⟷	21	22	23	24	25	26	27	Mishpatim* Shekalim (0)	
	14	15	16	17	18	19	20	⟷	28	29	30	1	2	3	4	Terumah	ADAR
	21	22	23	24	25	26	27	⟷	5	6	7	8	9	10	11	Tetzavveh Zachor (0)	
	28	1	2	3	4	5	6	⟷	12	13 Fast Esther	14 Purim	15 Shushan Purim	16	17	18	Ki Tissa Parah (0)	
MARCH	7	8	9	10	11	12	13	⟷	19	20	21	22	23	24	25	Vayakhel-Pekude* Hahodesh (0)	
	14	15	16	17	18	19	20	⟷	26	27	28	29	1	2	3	Vayikra	
	21	22	23	24	25	26	27	⟷	4	5	6	7	8	9	10	Tzav Haggadol (0)	
	28	29	30	31	1	2	3	⟷	11	12	13	14	15 Pesah	16 Pesah	17 Hol Hamoed	Hol Hamoed Pesah	NISAN
APRIL	4	5	6	7	8	9	10	⟷	18 Hol Hamoed	19 Hol Hamoed	20 Hol Hamoed	21 Pesah	22 Pesah	23	24	Shemini*	
	11	12	13	14	15	16	17	⟷	25	26	27	28	29	30	1	Tazria Metzora (1)	
	18	19	20	21	22	23	24	⟷	2	3	4	5	6	7	8	Ahare Kedoshim (8)	IYAR
	25	26	27	28	29	30	1	⟷	9	10	11	12	13	14	15	Emor	
MAY	2	3	4	5	6	7	8	⟷	16	17	18 Lag Baomer	19	20	21	22	Behar Behukkotai (0)	
	9	10	11	12	13	14	15	⟷	23	24	25	26	27	28	29	Bemidbar* (2)	
	16	17	18	19	20	21	22	⟷	1	2	3	4	5	6 Shavuoth	7 Shavuoth	Shavuoth II	SIVAN
	23	24	25	26	27	28	29	⟷	8	9	10	11	12	13	14	Naso	
	30	31	1	2	3	4	5	⟷	15	16	17	18	19	20	21	Behaalot' cha	
JUNE	6	7	8	9	10	11	12	⟷	22	23	24	25	26	27	28	Shelah L'cha*	
	13	14	15	16	17	18	19	⟷	29	30	1	2	3	4	5	Korah	

1999

CIVIL CALENDAR								HEBREW CALENDAR								
	SUN	MON	TUE	WED	THU	FRI	SAT		SUN	MON	TUE	WED	THU	FRI	SAT	SABBATH
JULY	20	21	22	23	24	25	26	⟷	6	7	8	9	10	11	12	Hukkath Balak (0)
	27	28	29	30	1	2	3	⟷	13	14	15	16	17 Fast Tammuz	18	19	Pin'has (0)
	4	5	6	7	8	9	10	⟷	20	21	22	23	24	25	26	Mattoth Mase (..)
	11	12	13	14	15	16	17	⟷	27	28	29	1	2	3	4	Devarim Hazon
AUGUST	18	19	20	21	22	23	24	⟷	5	6	7	8	9 Fast Ab	10	11	Vaetharan Naham.t
	25	26	27	28	29	30	31	⟷	12	13	14	15	16	17	18	Ekev
	1	2	3	4	5	6	7	⟷	19	20	21	22	23	24	25	Reeh*
	8	9	10	11	12	13	14	⟷	26	27	28	29	30	1	2	Shof'tim
	15	16	17	18	19	20	21	⟷	3	4	5	6	7	8	9	Ki Tetze
	22	23	24	25	26	27	28	⟷	10	11	12	13	14	15	16	Ki Tavo
SEPTEMBER	29	30	31	1	2	3	4	⟷	17	18	19	20	21	22	23	Nitzavim (0) Vayelech
	5	6	7	8	9	10	11	⟷	24	25	26	27	28	29	1 Rosh Hashanah	Rosh Hashanah I
	12	13	14	15	16	17	18	⟷	2 Rosh Hashanah	3 Fast Gedaliah	4	5	6	7	8	Haaz.nu Shuvah 12)
	19	20	21	22	23	24	25	⟷	9	10 Yom Kippur	11	12	13	14	15 Succoth	Succoth I
OCTOBER	26	27	28	29	30	1	2	⟷	16 Succoth	17 Hol Hamoed	18 Hol Hamoed	19 Hol Hamoed	20 Hol Hamoed	21 Hosh. Rabba	22 Shemini Atzereth	Shemini Atzereth
	3	4	5	6	7	8	9	⟷	23 Simhath Torah	24	25	26	27	28	29	Bereshith* (2)
	10	11	12	13	14	15	16	⟷	30	1	2	3	4	5	6	Noah
	17	18	19	20	21	22	23	⟷	7	8	9	10	11	12	13	Lech L.cha
	24	25	26	27	28	29	30	⟷	14	15	16	17	18	19	20	Vayera
NOVEMBER	31	1	2	3	4	5	6	⟷	21	22	23	24	25	26	27	Haye Sarah*
	7	8	9	10	11	12	13	⟷	28	29	30	1	2	3	4	ToFedth
	14	15	16	17	18	19	20	⟷	5	6	7	8	9	10	11	Vayetze
	21	22	23	24	25	26	27	⟷	12	13	14	15	16	17	18	Vay-shlah
	28	29	30	1	2	3	4	⟷	19	20	21	22	23	24	25 Hanukah	Vayeshev* (5)
DECEMBER	5	6	7	8	9	10	11	⟷	26 Hanukah	27 Hanukah	28 Hanukah	29 Hanukah	30 Hanukah	1 Hanukah	2 Hanukah	Mketz (6)
	12	13	14	15	16	17	18	⟷	3	4	5	6	7	8	9	Vaiggash
	19	20	21	22	23	24	25	⟷	10 Fast Tebeth	11	12	13	14	15	16	Va-hi

5759

TAMMUZ · AB · ELLUL · TISHRI · HESHVAN · KISLEV · TEBETH

2000		CIVIL CALENDAR								HEBREW CALENDAR								5760
		SUN	MON	TUE	WED	THU	FRI	SAT		SUN	MON	TUE	WED	THU	FRI	SAT	SABBATH	
		26	27	28	29	30	31	1	⟷	17	18	19	20	21	22	23	Shemoth*	
	JANUARY	2	3	4	5	6	7	8	⟷	24	25	26	27	28	29	1	Vaera (1)	SHEBAT
		9	10	11	12	13	14	15	⟷	2	3	4	5	6	7	8	Bo	
		16	17	18	19	20	21	22	⟷	9	10	11	12	13	14	15 Ham. Asar	Beshallah Shirah	
		23	24	25	26	27	28	29	⟷	16	17	18	19	20	21	22	Yithro	
		30	31	1	2	3	4	5	⟷	23	24	25	26	27	28	29	Mishpatim* (2)	
	FEBRUARY	6	7	8	9	10	11	12	⟷	30	1	2	3	4	5	6	Terumah	ADAR I
		13	14	15	16	17	18	19	⟷	7	8	9	10	11	12	13	Tetzavveh	
		20	21	22	23	24	25	26	⟷	14	15	16	17	18	19	20	Ki Tissa	
		27	28	29	1	2	3	4	⟷	21	22	23	24	25	26	27	Vayakhel* Shekalim (0)	
	MARCH	5	6	7	8	9	10	11	⟷	28	29	30	1	2	3	4	Pekude (6)	AD. II
		12	13	14	15	16	17	18	⟷	5	6	7	8	9	10	11	Vayikra Zachor (0)	
		19	20	21	22	23	24	25	⟷	12	13 Fast Esther	14 Purim	15 Shushan Purim	16	17	18	Tzav Parah (0)	
		26	27	28	29	30	31	1	⟷	19	20	21	22	23	24	25	Shemini* Hahodesh (0)	
	APRIL	2	3	4	5	6	7	8	⟷	26	27	28	29	1	2	3	Tazria	NISAN
		9	10	11	12	13	14	15	⟷	4	5	6	7	8	9	10	Metzora Haggadol (0)	
		16	17	18	19	20	21	22	⟷	11	12	13	14	15 Pesah	16 Pesah	17 Hol Hamoed	Hol Hamoed Pesah	
		23	24	25	26	27	28	29	⟷	18 Hol Hamoed	19 Hol Hamoed	20 Hol Hamoed	21 Pesah	22 Pesah	23	24	Ahare* (7)	
		30	1	2	3	4	5	6	⟷	25	26	27	28	29	30	1	Kedoshim (1)	
	MAY	7	8	9	10	11	12	13	⟷	2	3	4	5	6	7	8	Emor	IYAR
		14	15	16	17	18	19	20	⟷	9	10	11	12	13	14	15	Behar	
		21	22	23	24	25	26	27	⟷	16	17	18 Lag Baomer	19	20	21	22	Behukkotai	
		28	29	30	31	1	2	3	⟷	23	24	25	26	27	28	29	Bemidbar* (2)	
	JUNE	4	5	6	7	8	9	10	⟷	1	2	3	4	5	6 Shavuoth	7 Shavuoth	Shavuoth II	SIVAN
		11	12	13	14	15	16	17	⟷	8	9	10	11	12	13	14	Naso	
		18	19	20	21	22	23	24	⟷	15	16	17	18	19	20	21	Behaalot'cha	
		25	26	27	28	29	30	1	⟷	22	23	24	25	26	27	28	Shelah L'cha*	

	CIVIL CALENDAR								HEBREW CALENDAR								
2000	SUN	MON	TUE	WED	THU	FRI	SAT		SUN	MON	TUE	WED	THU	FRI	SAT	SABBATH	**5760**
JULY	2	3	4	5	6	7	8	⟷	29	30	1	2	3	4	5	Korah	TAMMUZ
	9	10	11	12	13	14	15	⟷	6	7	8	9	10	11	12	Hukkath Balak (0)	
	16	17	18	19	20	21	22	⟷	13	14	15	16	17 Fast Tammuz	18	19	Pin'has (10)	
	23	24	25	26	27	28	29	⟷	20	21	22	23	24	25	26	Mattoth* Mase (11)	
	30	31	1	2	3	4	5	⟷	27	28	29	1	2	3	4	Devarim Hazon	
AUGUST	6	7	8	9	10	11	12	⟷	5	6	7	8	9 Fast Ab	10	11	Vaethanan Nahamu	AB
	13	14	15	16	17	18	19	⟷	12	13	14	15	16	17	18	Ekev	
	20	21	22	23	24	25	26	⟷	19	20	21	22	23	24	25	Reeh*	
	27	28	29	30	31	1	2	⟷	26	27	28	29	30	1	2	Shof'tim	
SEPTEMBER	3	4	5	6	7	8	9	⟷	3	4	5	6	7	8	9	Ki Tetze	ELLUL
	10	11	12	13	14	15	16	⟷	10	11	12	13	14	15	16	Ki Tavo	
	17	18	19	20	21	22	23	⟷	17	18	19	20	21	22	23	Nitzavim(0) Vayelech	
	24	25	26	27	28	29	30	⟷	24	25	26	27	28	29	1 Rosh Hashanah	Rosh Hashanah I	
OCTOBER	1	2	3	4	5	6	7	⟷	2 Rosh Hashanah	3 Fast Gedaliah	4	5	6	7	8	Haazinu Shuvah (2)	TISHRI
	8	9	10	11	12	13	14	⟷	9	10 Yom Kippur	11	12	13	14	15 Succoth	Succoth	
	15	16	17	18	19	20	21	⟷	16 Succoth	17 Hol Hamoed	18 Hol Hamoed	19 Hol Hamoed	20 Hol Hamoed	21 Rosh Rabba	22 Shemini Atzereth	Shemini Atzereth	
	22	23	24	25	26	27	28	⟷	23 Simhath Torah	24	25	26	27	28	29	Bereshith (2)	
	29	30	31	1	2	3	4	⟷	30	1	2	3	4	5	6	Noah	
NOVEMBER	5	6	7	8	9	10	11	⟷	7	8	9	10	11	12	13	Lech L'cha	HESHVAN
	12	13	14	15	16	17	18	⟷	14	15	16	17	18	19	20	Vayera	
	19	20	21	22	23	24	25	⟷	21	22	23	24	25	26	27	Haye Sara*	
	26	27	28	29	30	1	2	⟷	28	29	1	2	3	4	5	Toi'doth	
DECEMBER	3	4	5	6	7	8	9	⟷	6	7	8	9	10	11	12	Vayetze	KISLEV
	10	11	12	13	14	15	16	⟷	13	14	15	16	17	18	19	Vayishlah	
	17	18	19	20	21	22	23	⟷	20	21	22	23	24	25 Hanukah	26 Hanukah	Vayeshev* (5)	
	24	25	26	27	28	29	30	⟷	27 Hanukah	28 Hanukah	29 Hanukah	1 Hanukah	2 Hanukah	3 Hanukah	4	Mikketz	

CIVIL CALENDAR								HEBREW CALENDAR								
2001 SUN	MON	TUE	WED	THU	FRI	SAT		SUN	MON	TUE	WED	THU	FRI	SAT	SABBATH	**5761**
31	1	2	3	4	5	6	⟷	5	6	7	8	9	10 Fast Tebeth	11	Vayiggash	TEBETH
7	8	9	10	11	12	13	⟷	12	13	14	15	16	17	18	Vayhi	
14	15	16	17	18	19	20	⟷	19	20	21	22	23	24	25	Shemoth°	
21	22	23	24	25	26	27	⟷	26	27	28	29	1	2	3	Vaera	
28	29	30	31	1	2	3	⟷	4	5	6	7	8	9	10	Bo	SHEBAT
4	5	6	7	8	9	10	⟷	11	12	13	14	15 Ham. Asar	16	17	Beshallah Shirah	
11	12	13	14	15	16	17	⟷	18	19	20	21	22	23	24	Yithro°	
18	19	20	21	22	23	24	⟷	25	26	27	28	29	30	1	Mishpatim Shekalim (O, 3)	ADAR
25	26	27	28	1	2	3	⟷	2	3	4	5	6	7	8	Terumah Zachor (O)	
4	5	6	7	8	9	10	⟷	9	10	11	12	13 Fast Esther	14 Purim	15 Shushan Purim	Tetzavveh	
11	12	13	14	15	16	17	⟷	16	17	18	19	20	21	22	Ki Tissa Parah (O)	
18	19	20	21	22	23	24	⟷	23	24	25	26	27	28	29	Vayakhel, Pekude° Hahodesh (O, 4)	
25	26	27	28	29	30	31	⟷	1	2	3	4	5	6	7	Vayikra	
1	2	3	4	5	6	7	⟷	8	9	10	11	12	13	14	Tzav Haggadol (O)	NISAN
8	9	10	11	12	13	14	⟷	15 Pesah	16 Pesah	17 Hol Hamoed	18 Hol Hamoed	19 Hol Hamoed	20 Hol Hamoed	21 Pesah	Pesah VII	
15	16	17	18	19	20	21	⟷	22 Pesah	23	24	25	26	27	28	Shemini°	
22	23	24	25	26	27	28	⟷	29	30	1	2	3	4	5	Tazria Metzora (O)	
29	30	1	2	3	4	5	⟷	6	7	8	9	10	11	12	Ahare Kedoshim (8)	IYAR
6	7	8	9	10	11	12	⟷	13	14	15	16	17	18 Lag Baomer	19	Emor	
13	14	15	16	17	18	19	⟷	20	21	22	23	24	25	26	Behar° Behukkotai (O)	
20	21	22	23	24	25	26	⟷	27	28	29	1	2	3	4	Bemidbar	
27	28	29	30	31	1	2	⟷	5	6 Shavuoth	7 Shavuoth	8	9	10	11	Naso	SIVAN
3	4	5	6	7	8	9	⟷	12	13	14	15	16	17	18	Behaalot'cha	
10	11	12	13	14	15	16	⟷	19	20	21	22	23	24	25	Shelah L'cha°	
17	18	19	20	21	22	23	⟷	26	27	28	29	30	1	2	Korah	
24	25	26	27	28	29	30	⟷	3	4	5	6	7	8	9	Hukkath	

Civil months (left, top to bottom): JANUARY, FEBRUARY, MARCH, APRIL, MAY, JUNE

CIVIL CALENDAR   HEBREW CALENDAR

2001   **5761**

	SUN	MON	TUE	WED	THU	FRI	SAT		SUN	MON	TUE	WED	THU	FRI	SAT	SABBATH	
JULY	1	2	3	4	5	6	7	⟷	10	11	12	13	14	15	16	Balak	**TAMMUZ**
	8	9	10	11	12	13	14	⟷	17 Fast Tammuz	18	19	20	21	22	23	Pin'has* (10)	
	15	16	17	18	19	20	21	⟷	24	25	26	27	28	29	1	Mattoth Mase (11, 3	
AUGUST	22	23	24	25	26	27	28	⟷	2	3	4	5	6	7	8	Devarim Hazon	**AB**
	29	30	31	1	2	3	4	⟷	9 Fast Ab	10	11	12	13	14	15	Vaethanan Nahamu	
	5	6	7	8	9	10	11	⟷	16	17	18	19	20	21	22	Ekev	
	12	13	14	15	16	17	18	⟷	23	24	25	26	27	28	29	Reeh* (4)	
	19	20	21	22	23	24	25	⟷	30	1	2	3	4	5	6	Shof'tim	**ELLUL**
SEP	26	27	28	29	30	31	1	⟷	7	8	9	10	11	12	13	Ki Tetze	
	2	3	4	5	6	7	8	⟷	14	15	16	17	18	19	20	Ki Tavo	
	9	10	11	12	13	14	15	⟷	21	22	23	24	25	26	27	Nitzavim	
SEP	16	17	18	19	20	21	22	⟷	28	29	1 Rosh Hashanah	2 Rosh Hashanah	3 Fast Gedaliah	4	5	Vayelech Shuvah (2)	**TISHRI**
	23	24	25	26	27	28	29	⟷	6	7	8	9	10 Yom Kippur	11	12	Haazinu	
OCTOBER	30	1	2	3	4	5	6	⟷	13	14	15 Succoth	16 Succoth	17 Hol Hamoed	18 Hol Hamoed	19 Hol Hamoed	Hol Hamoed Succoth	
	7	8	9	10	11	12	13	⟷	20 Hol Hamoed	21 Hosh. Rabba	22 Shemini Atzereth	23 Simhath Torah	24	25	26	Bereshith*	
	14	15	16	17	18	19	20	⟷	27	28	29	30	1	2	3	Noah	**HESHVAN**
	21	22	23	24	25	26	27	⟷	4	5	6	7	8	9	10	Lech L'caa	
NOVEMBER	28	29	30	31	1	2	3	⟷	11	12	13	14	15	16	17	Vayera	
	4	5	6	7	8	9	10	⟷	18	19	20	21	22	23	24	Haye Sarah*	
	11	12	13	14	15	16	17	⟷	25	26	27	28	29	1	2	Tol'doth	**KISLEV**
	18	19	20	21	22	23	24	⟷	3	4	5	6	7	8	9	Vayetze	
DECEMBER	25	26	27	28	29	30	1	⟷	10	11	12	13	14	15	16	Vayish ah	
	2	3	4	5	6	7	8	⟷	17	18	19	20	21	22	23	Vayeshev*	
	9	10	11	12	13	14	15	⟷	24	25 Hanukah	26 Hanukah	27 Hanukah	28 Hanukah	29 Hanukah	30 Hanukah	Mikketz (5, 3, 4)	**TEBETH**
	16	17	18	19	20	21	22	⟷	1 Hanukah	2 Hanukah	3	4	5	6	7	Vayiggash	
	23	24	25	26	27	28	29	⟷	8	9	10 Fast Tebeth	11	12	13	14	Vayhi	

2002 · CIVIL CALENDAR — HEBREW CALENDAR · **5762**

Month	SUN	MON	TUE	WED	THU	FRI	SAT		SUN	MON	TUE	WED	THU	FRI	SAT	SABBATH	Heb. Month
JANUARY	30	31	1	2	3	4	5	⟷	15	16	17	18	19	20	21	Shemoth	TEBETH
	6	7	8	9	10	11	12	⟷	22	23	24	25	26	27	28	Vaera*	
	13	14	15	16	17	18	19	⟷	29	1	2	3	4	5	6	Bo	SHEBAT
	20	21	22	23	24	25	26	⟷	7	8	9	10	11	12	13	Beshallah Shirah	
	27	28	29	30	31	1	2	⟷	14	15 (Ham. Asar)	16	17	18	19	20	Yithro	
FEBRUARY	3	4	5	6	7	8	9	⟷	21	22	23	24	25	26	27	Mishpatim* Shekalim (O)	
	10	11	12	13	14	15	16	⟷	28	29	30	1	2	3	4	Terumah	ADAR
	17	18	19	20	21	22	23	⟷	5	6	7	8	9	10	11	Tetzavveh Zachor (O)	
	24	25	26	27	28	1	2	⟷	12	13 (Fast Esther)	14 (Purim)	15 (Shushan Purim)	16	17	18	Ki Tissa Parah (O)	
MARCH	3	4	5	6	7	8	9	⟷	19	20	21	22	23	24	25	Vayakhel-Pekude* Hahodesh (O)	
	10	11	12	13	14	15	16	⟷	26	27	28	29	1	2	3	Vayikra	NISAN
	17	18	19	20	21	22	23	⟷	4	5	6	7	8	9	10	Tzav Haggadol (O)	
	24	25	26	27	28	29	30	⟷	11	12	13	14	15 (Pesah)	16 (Pesah)	17 (Hol Hamoed)	Hol Hamoed Pesah	
APRIL	31	1	2	3	4	5	6	⟷	18 (Hol Hamoed)	19 (Hol Hamoed)	20 (Hol Hamoed)	21 (Pesah)	22 (Pesah)	23	24	Shemini*	
	7	8	9	10	11	12	13	⟷	25	26	27	28	29	30	1	Tazria Metzora (1)	IYAR
	14	15	16	17	18	19	20	⟷	2	3	4	5	6	7	8	Ahare Kedoshim (8)	
	21	22	23	24	25	26	27	⟷	9	10	11	12	13	14	15	Emor	
	28	29	30	1	2	3	4	⟷	16	17	18 (Lag Baomer)	19	20	21	22	Behar Behukkotai (O)	
MAY	5	6	7	8	9	10	11	⟷	23	24	25	26	27	28	29	Bemidbar* (2)	
	12	13	14	15	16	17	18	⟷	1	2	3	4	5	6 (Shavuoth)	7 (Shavuoth)	Shavuoth II	SIVAN
	19	20	21	22	23	24	25	⟷	8	9	10	11	12	13	14	Naso	
	26	27	28	29	30	31	1	⟷	15	16	17	18	19	20	21	Behaalot'cha	
JUNE	2	3	4	5	6	7	8	⟷	22	23	24	25	26	27	28	Shelah Lecha*	
	9	10	11	12	13	14	15	⟷	29	30	1	2	3	4	5	Korah	
	16	17	18	19	20	21	22	⟷	6	7	8	9	10	11	12	Hukkath Balak (O)	TAMMUZ
	23	24	25	26	27	28	29	⟷	13	14	15	16	17 (Fast Tammuz)	18	19	Pin'has (10)	
	30	1	2	3	4	5	6	⟷	20	21	22	23	24	25	26	Mattoth* Mase (11)	

2002 — CIVIL CALENDAR / HEBREW CALENDAR — 5763

	CIVIL CALENDAR SUN MON TUE WED THU FRI SAT		HEBREW CALENDAR SUN MON TUE WED THU FRI SAT	SABBATH	
JULY	7 8 9 10 11 12 13	⟷	27 28 29 1 2 3 4	Devarim Hazon	
	14 15 16 17 18 19 20	⟷	5 6 7 8 9 (Fast Ab) 10 11	Vaethanan Nahamu	AB
	21 22 23 24 25 26 27	⟷	12 13 14 15 16 17 18	Ekev	
	28 29 30 31 1 2 3	⟷	19 20 21 22 23 24 25	Reeh*	
AUGUST	4 5 6 7 8 9 10	⟷	26 27 28 29 30 1 2	Shof'tim	
	11 12 13 14 15 16 17	⟷	3 4 5 6 7 8 9	Ki Tetze	ELLUL
	18 19 20 21 22 23 24	⟷	10 11 12 13 14 15 16	Ki Tavo	
	25 26 27 28 29 30 31	⟷	17 18 19 20 21 22 23	Nitzavim (30) Vayelech	
SEPTEMBER	1 2 3 4 5 6 7	⟷	24 25 26 27 28 29 1 (Rosh Hashanah)	Rosh Hashanah I	
	8 9 10 11 12 13 14	⟷	2 (Rosh Hashanah) 3 (Fast Gedaliah) 4 5 6 7 8	Haazinu Shuvah (12)	TISHRI
	15 16 17 18 19 20 21	⟷	9 10 (Yom Kippur) 11 12 13 14 15 (Succoth)	Succoth I	
	22 23 24 25 26 27 28	⟷	16 (Succoth) 17 (Hol Hamoed) 18 (Hol Hamoed) 19 (Hol Hamoed) 20 (Hol Hamoed) 21 (Hosh. Rabba) 22 (Shemini Atzereth)	Shemini Azzereth	
	29 30 1 2 3 4 5	⟷	23 (Simhath Torah) 24 25 26 27 28 29	Bereshith* (2)	
OCTOBER	6 7 8 9 10 11 12	⟷	30 1 2 3 4 5 6	Noah	
	13 14 15 16 17 18 19	⟷	7 8 9 10 11 12 13	Lech L'cha	HESHVAN
	20 21 22 23 24 25 26	⟷	14 15 16 17 18 19 20	Vayera	
	27 28 29 30 31 1 2	⟷	21 22 23 24 25 26 27	Haye Sarah*	
NOVEMBER	3 4 5 6 7 8 9	⟷	28 29 30 1 2 3 4	Tol'doth	
	10 11 12 13 14 15 16	⟷	5 6 7 8 9 10 11	Vayetze	KISLEV
	17 18 19 20 21 22 23	⟷	12 13 14 15 16 17 18	Vayishlah	
	24 25 26 27 28 29 30	⟷	19 20 21 22 23 24 25 (Hanukah)	Vayeshev* (5)	
DECEMBER	1 2 3 4 5 6 7	⟷	26 (Hanukah) 27 (Hanukah) 28 (Hanukah) 29 (Hanukah) 30 (Hanukah) 1 (Hanukah) 2 (Hanukah)	Mikketz (6)	
	8 9 10 11 12 13 14	⟷	3 4 5 6 7 8 9	Vayiggash	TEBETH
	15 16 17 18 19 20 21	⟷	10 (Fast Tebeth) 11 12 13 14 15 16	Vayhi	
	22 23 24 25 26 27 28	⟷	17 18 19 20 21 22 23	Shemot*